HIGHER EDUCATION TAX CREDITS AND DEDUCTIONS

HIGHER EDUCATION TAX CREDITS AND DEDUCTIONS

ADAM STOLL AND JAMES B. STEDMAN

Novinka Books
New York

Senior Editors: Susan Boriotti and Donna Dennis
Coordinating Editor: Tatiana Shohov
Office Manager: Annette Hellinger
Graphics: Wanda Serrano
Editorial Production: Maya Columbus, Vladimir Klestov, Matthew Kozlowski, Tom Moceri and Anthony T. Sovak
Circulation: Ave Maria Gonzalez, Vera Popovic, Luis Aviles, Raymond Davis, Melissa Diaz and Jeannie Pappas
Communications and Acquisitions: Serge P. Shohov

Library of Congress Cataloging-in-Publication Data
Available Upon Request

ISBN 1-59033-607-0

Copyright © 2003 by Novinka Books, An Imprint of
Nova Science Publishers, Inc.
400 Oser Ave, Suite 1600
Hauppauge, New York 11788-3619
Tele.: 631-231-7269   Fax: 631-231-8175
e-mail: Novascience@earthlink.net
Web Site: http://www.novapublishers.com

All rights reserved. No part of this book may be reproduced, stored in a retrieval system or transmitted in any form or by any means: electronic, electrostatic, magnetic, tape, mechanical photocopying, recording or otherwise without permission from the publishers.

The authors and publisher have taken care in preparation of this book, but make no expressed or implied warranty of any kind and assume no responsibility for any errors or omissions. No liability is assumed for incidental or consequential damages in connection with or arising out of information contained in this book.

This publication is designed to provide accurate and authoritative information with regard to the subject matter covered herein. It is sold with the clear understanding that the publisher is not engaged in rendering legal or any other professional services. If legal or any other expert assistance is required, the services of a competent person should be sought. FROM A DECLARATION OF PARTICIPANTS JOINTLY ADOPTED BY A COMMITTEE OF THE AMERICAN BAR ASSOCIATION AND A COMMITTEE OF PUBLISHERS.

Printed in the United States of America

CONTENTS

Preface vii

Chapter 1 Higher Education Tax Credits and Deduction: An Overview of the Benefits and their Relationship to Traditional Student Aid 1

Chapter 2 Higher Education Tax Credits: Targeting Value, and Interaction with Other Federal Student Aid 21

Index 71

PREFACE

This book provides background information for the Higher Education Act (HEA) reauthorization process about the direct assistance for education expenses provided through the federal income tax system. Key features of the benefits are explored. Also explored is the relationship of the traditional student aid delivery system with the tax system as a conduit for postsecondary education assistance, identifying specific issues that may be important for congressional consideration during HEA reauthorization. It also presents newly generated estimates of the value of the credits available to varied eligible recipients. In the absence of actual data, modeling approaches that simulate tax credit values offer perhaps the most promising way to examine the targeting of the education tax credits. Two different modeling approaches are applied in the analysis presented in this book.

Chapter 1

HIGHER EDUCATION TAX CREDITS AND DEDUCTION: AN OVERVIEW OF THE BENEFITS AND THEIR RELATIONSHIP TO TRADITIONAL STUDENT AID

SUMMARY

The Taxpayer Relief Act of 1997 established two federal income tax credits for qualified postsecondary education expenses – The Hope Scholarship tax credit and the Lifetime Learning tax credit. The Economic Growth and Tax Relief Reconciliation Act of 2001 established. a new tax deduction for higher education expenses beginning in 2002.

The Hope credit was introduced to help ensure that students have access to the first 2 years of undergraduate postsecondary education. The Lifetime Learning credit and new tax deduction provide support for students in any year of study in undergraduate and graduate programs. Additionally, the Lifetime Learning credit and new tax deduction occupy a unique niche as widely available assistance for individuals taking occasional courses. Middle and upper-middle income individuals are the targeted beneficiaries of each of these higher education tax benefits.

Key features of the credits and the new deduction largely dictate who these provisions benefit and the amount of aid they will receive. Among these are limits on maximum benefits, the nonrefundable nature of the credits, income thresholds for phasing out the benefits, and the type of school enrollment covered by benefits.

The Hope credit, a nonrefundable credit for the tuition and fees required for enrollment that are not offset by grant aid, has a maximum value of 1,500. The Lifetime credit, also nonrefundable tax credit, has a maximum value of $1,000. The new deduction permits deduction of qualified expenses of up to $3,000 for 2002 and 2003, and up to 4,000 for 2004 and 2005. The value of the tax deduction will depend, in part on taxpayers marginal tax rates. At specified thresholds of modified adjusted gross income, the tax benefits phase out. These thresholds are identical for the tax credits, and higher for tax deduction.

With the introduction of these tax benefits, individual can now receive substantial amounts of federal financial assistance for postsecondary education from two parallel systems – the federal income tax system and traditional student aid delivery system, which provides aid such as grants, loans, or work opportunities. The traditional system helps students meet current expenses; the tax system requires families to make higher education outlays that are reimbursed through tax reductions determined near the end of or after an academic year. Tax benefits may offer streamlined delivery of aid, while most other aid is delivered through relatively cumbersome and labor-intensive processes. Some criticize the complexity of the tax process, which adds another system that students and families must navigate. Institutional reporting requirements associated with the tax benefits are viewed by many in the higher education community as burdensome and expensive. P.L. 107-131 (signed into law on January 16, 2002) modifies some of the reporting requirements.

INTRODUCTION

The Taxpayer Relief Act of 1997 (TRA, P.L. 105-34) established two federal income tax credits for qualified postsecondary education expenses — the Hope Scholarship tax credit and the Lifetime Learning tax credit. In 2001, the Economic Growth and Tax Relief Reconciliation Act of 2001 (P.L. 107-16) established a new tax deduction for higher education expenses beginning in 2002.[1] The value of these benefits in foregone federal revenue places them among the largest sources of federal support to meet the costs of postsecondary education. Preliminary data from the Internal Revenue

---

[1] This chapter does not address other tax provisions intended to help families meet their postsecondary education expenses through savings, such as the Federal Coverdell education savings accounts. See CRS Report RS20289, Education Savings Accounts for Elementary and Secondary Education, by Bob Lyke and James Stedman.

Service (IRS) for 1999 show that in that tax year 6.5 million returns claimed $4.8 billion in education tax credits.[2]

At present there are two parallel systems through which the federal government provides assistance for postsecondary education attendance—the traditional student aid delivery system and the federal income tax system. With the anticipated expiration of the funding authority for Higher Education Act (HEA) programs during the 108th Congress, the Congress will be considering the amendment and extension of major federal aid programs under HEA Title IV that use the traditional delivery system; among these programs are the Pell Grant program (an estimated $9.2 billion in grant aid for FY2001) and the Federal Family Education Loan and Direct Loan programs (an estimated $34.8 billion in new loan volume for FY2001).[3]

This chapter is intended to provide background information for the HEA reauthorization process about the direct assistance for education expenses provided through the federal income tax system, thereby placing the congressional consideration of the HEA student aid programs in a broader context. Although data on the actual use and impact of the tax credits are scarce, key aspects of the form and function of these credits and the new deduction dictate, to a large degree, who these tax provisions benefit and by how much. These key features of the benefits are explored in this chapter. Further, it explores the relationship of the traditional student aid delivery system with the tax system as a conduit for postsecondary education assistance, identifying specific issues that may be important for congressional consideration during HEA reauthorization.

An important distinction underlies this chapter — the tax system as a mechanism for providing benefits for postsecondary education expenses differs in significant ways from the traditional student aid delivery system. Tax benefits flow through a system that is dependent upon individuals' tax status and the level of qualified higher education expenses incurred. The tax benefit calculations are independent of any direct measurement of the ability to pay for postsecondary education. Further, these benefits are not subject to annual appropriations. In contrast, federal assistance provided through the traditional delivery system consists of grant, loan, and work aid. Much of this aid is awarded directly to students while some is controlled and disbursed by financial aid officers at postsecondary institutions. A significant

---

[2] Balkovic, Brian. Internal Revenue Service. Individual Income Tax Returns, Preliminary Data, 1999. Statistics of Income Bulletin. Spring 2001. Downloaded from the IRS web site, [http://www.irs.treas.gov/], August 31,2001. (Hereafter cited as IRS, Individual Income Tax Returns.)

[3] Only somewhat less than 40% of the new loan volume consists of federal funds; the remainder is private capital supported by federal loan guarantees and subsidies.

portion of this assistance is awarded on the basis of students' financial need.[4] Finally, a significant portion of this assistance is subject to annual appropriations.

FORM-AN OVERVIEW OF THE BENEFITS[5]

Hope Scholarship Credit

The Hope Scholarship credit is a nonrefundable credit against federal income tax liability for qualified tuition and related higher education expenses.[6] At present, the credit *for each eligible student* is 100% of the first $1,000 of qualified tuition and related expenses and 50% of the second $1,000 of such expenses, for a maximum of $1,500. After tax year 2001, the maximum Hope credit will be indexed for inflation.

Taxpayers can claim the credit for qualified higher education expenses paid for eligible students—including the taxpayers themselves, their spouse, and dependents for whom they claim tax exemptions.[7] A taxpayer can claim a credit with respect to each eligible student. Eligible students must have been enrolled on at least a half-time basis for at least one academic period during the tax year in a higher education program leading to a degree, certificate, or credential. They cannot have finished the first 2 years of undergraduate education and the credit can only be claimed for their first 2 years. Individuals with a federal or state felony conviction for drug possession or distribution are not eligible for the credit.

Qualified tuition and related expenses are tuition and fees required for enrollment at institutions eligible to participate in U.S. Department of Education (ED) student aid programs, including accredited public, private,

---

[4] While still dominant, the portion of student aid that is being awarded dependent on need may be declining. As reported by the Advisory Committee on Student Financial Assistance, "At the state level, new grant aid has shifted steadily in favor of merit-based aid and against need-based aid." *(Access Denied: Restoring the Nation's Commitment to Equal Educational Opportunity,* February 2001, p. 8.) The Committee reports that 18.6% of state grant aid funds are now merit-based.

[5] See also CRS Report 97-915, Tax Benefits for Education in the Taxpayer Relief Act of 1997: New Legislative Developments, by Bob Lyke.

[6] Only individuals with income tax liability can benefit from a nonrefundable tax credit. Unlike a deduction, which reduces the amount of income subject to tax, a credit directly reduces the tax itself. A nonrefundable credit cannot be worth more than the amount of the tax. For a taxpayer with a refundable tax credit that exceeds tax liability, a payment is made by the federal government to the taxpayer in the amount of the difference.

[7] Expenses paid by a dependent or someone other than the filer, spouse, or dependent are treated as if paid by the taxpayer.

and proprietary postsecondary institutions. Eligible expenses include those fees required as a condition for enrollment.[8] Room and board expenses are not included. Qualified higher education expenses are reduced by the amount of non-taxable educational assistance (exclusive of loans and gifts) received by a qualified student. This includes education assistance that is excluded from taxpayers' gross income, including Pell Grants, scholarships, veterans' educational benefits, and employer-provided tuition reimbursements.

The Hope tax credit begins to be phased out for individuals as modified adjusted gross income[9] increases beyond $40,000 and is completely phased out at $50,000 (for those filing joint returns, the income thresholds are $80,000 and $100,000).[10] These various income thresholds will be indexed to inflation beginning after tax year 2001.

The Hope credit cannot be claimed for a student if the Lifetime Learning credit is claimed for the same tax year for that same student. Individuals for whom a Hope credit is claimed cannot concurrently benefit from the deduction for qualified higher education expenses.

Lifetime Learning Credit

The Lifetime Learning credit is also a nonrefundable tax credit for qualified tuition and related higher education expenses. Currently, the credit per tax return is 20% of the first $5,000 of qualified higher education expenses, for a maximum of $1,000. For qualified expenses paid after December 31, 2002, the credit will be a maximum of $2,000, calculated as 20% of the first $10,000 in qualified expenses.

As with the Hope credit, taxpayers can claim the Lifetime Learning credit for the qualified higher education expenses paid for eligible students — including the taxpayers themselves, their spouse, and dependents for

---

[8] Fees for course-related books, supplies, and equipment and activity fees are included only if they are paid to the institution as a condition of enrollment.

[9] In general, taxpayers' modified adjusted gross income will equal their adjusted gross income. For taxpayers who exclude income earned abroad or from certain U.S. territories or possessions, modified adjusted gross income is their adjusted gross income increased by those excluded amounts.

[10] A formula adjusts the credit values for income of less than the ceiling but more than the threshold for receiving the full benefit: the modified adjusted gross income is subtracted from the income ceiling, the remainder is divided by $10,000 ($20,000 for joint returns) and then multiplied by the originally calculated credit value to produce an adjusted credit value. For example, for a taxpayer filing a joint return with modified adjusted gross income of $90,000 and a tentative Hope credit of $1,500, the Hope credit would be reduced by half to $750 ($100,000 - $90,000 = $10,000; $10,000/$20,000 = .50; $1,500 x .50 = $750).

whom they claim tax exemptions. Eligible students are those enrolled in one or more courses of undergraduate or graduate instruction to acquire or improve job skills. There is no limit on the number of years for which the credit may be claimed.

Qualified tuition and related expenses are calculated and treated in the same fashion as they are under the Hope credits, including the reduction for nontaxable educational assistance received.

As with the Hope tax credit, the Lifetime Learning credit begins to be phased out as modified adjusted gross income increases beyond $40,000 and is completely phased out at $50,000 (for individuals filing joint returns, the income thresholds are $80,000 and $100,000).[11] These various income thresholds will be indexed to inflation beginning after tax year 2001.

The Lifetime Learning credit cannot be claimed for a student if the Hope credit is claimed for the same tax year for that same student. Individuals for whom a Lifetime Learning credit is claimed cannot concurrently benefit from the tax deduction for qualified higher education expenses.

Higher Education Deduction

The Economic Growth and Tax Relief Reconciliation Act of 2001 (P.L. 107-16) establishes a new above-the-line deduction for taxpayers who pay qualified higher education expenses.[12] It is terminated for tax years beginning after December 31, 2005.

In 2002 and 2003, the maximum deduction permitted per *return* is $3,000. This deduction can be taken by individuals with modified adjusted gross income of up to $65,000. For filers of joint returns, the deduction is available for those with modified adjusted gross income of up to $130,000. For 2004 and 2005, the maximum deduction rises to $4,000 with the same income limits. A smaller deduction of $2,000 is provided for 2004 and 2005 for taxpayers whose modified adjusted gross income is more than $65,000 but not more than $80,000 (for those filing joint returns, more than $130,000 but not more than $160,000). How much the deduction win be worth to a taxpayer depends upon a variety of factors, including the

---

[11] Lifetime Learning credits are phased out by same formula applied to Hope credits when income is higher than the threshold for the full credit but less than the threshold for complete elimination of the credit.

[12] An above-the-line deduction is taken against a taxpayer's gross income, directly affecting the calculation of adjusted gross income. This deduction can be taken regardless of whether the taxpayer itemizes deductions.

taxpayer's marginal tax rate.[13] The higher education deduction reduces a taxpayer's adjusted gross income dollar for dollar. Depending upon the taxpayer's marginal tax rate that reduction is worth different amounts. For example, for a taxpayer in the 15% tax bracket with $3,000 in qualified expenses in 2002 or 2003, the tax benefit would be $450 in reduced tax liability.[14] For an individual in the 27% tax bracket with $3,000 in qualified expenses, the $3,000 tax deduction would be worth $810.[15]

Taxpayers can take the deduction if they pay the qualified higher education expenses for themselves, spouses, or dependents for whom tax exemptions are claimed.[16] There are no limitations on the level of postsecondary education enrollment (undergraduate and graduate enrollment is covered) or the intensity of enrollment (eligible expenses related to just a single course of study are covered).

The qualified higher education expenses for the deduction are defined as they are for the Hope and Lifetime Learning credits. Qualified higher education expenses appear to be reduced in the same fashion as they are for the credits.

The deduction cannot be taken for the qualified higher education expenses for any individual for whom the Hope or Lifetime Learning credits are claimed.

Major Features of the Tax Benefits

Table 1, below, provides an overview of the major features of each of these three tax benefits.

---

[13] The marginal tax rate is the tax rate applied to the last additional dollar of income.
[14] The calculation is as follows: 15% of $3,000 = $450 maximum in tax savings.
[15] The calculation is as follows: 27% of $3,000 = $810 maximum in tax savings. The statutory rates of 15% and 27% used in this example are the marginal rates that will usually apply to the majority of middle income parents in tax years 2001-2003.
[16] Based on the statutory provisions in P.L. 107-16, the broader provisions of the Hope and Lifetime Learning credits concerning payments made by dependents or someone other than the filer do not appear to apply to the deduction.

Table 1. Major Features of the Hope Scholarship Credit, Lifetime Learning Credit, and Higher Education Tax Deduction

Feature	Hope Scholarship Credit	Lifetime Learning Credit	Higher Education tax deduction
Type of benefit	Nonrefundable tax credit (cannot exceed tax liability)	Nonrefundable tax credit (cannot exceed tax liability)	Above the line tax deduction (filers do not need to itemize)
Maximum benefit	$1,500 (100% of first $1,000 in qualified expenses, 50% of second $1,000) per student through tax year 2001; after which the maximum Hope credit will be indexed for inflation	$1000 (20% of first $5,000 in qualified expenses) per return through tax year 2002; after which the credit will be a maximum of $2,000 (20% of first $10,000 in qualified expenses)	$3,000 deduction for 2002 and 2003 per return; $4,000 deduction for 2004 and 2005 per return ($2,000 maximum deduction for 2004 and 2005 available for higher income taxpayers). Note: value of the maximum deduction depends upon taxpayer's marginal tax rate
Income limit	Credit begins to phase out at $40,000 modified adjusted gross income and is fully phased out at $50,000 ($80,000 and $100,000 thresholds for joint returns) Income levels indexed to inflation effective tax year 2002	Credit begins to phase out at $40,000 modified adjusted gross income and is fully phased out at $50,000 ($80,000 and $100,000 thresholds for joint returns) Income levels indexed to inflation effective tax year 2002	For 2002 through 2005, deduction available to taxpayers with up to $65,000 in modified adjusted gross income ($130,000 for joint returns); for 2004 or 2005, taxpayers with modified adjusted gross income of more than $65,000 but less than $80,000 can claim a smaller maximum deduction ($130,000 and $160,000 thresholds for joint returns)
Post-secondary education expenses qualifying for benefit	Tuition and fees required for enrollment	Tuition and fees required for enrollment	Tuition and fees required for enrollment
Type of post-secondary education	First 2 years of undergraduate education when enrolled on at least a half-time basis in a program leading to a degree, credential, or certificate	For any year of undergraduate or graduate enrollment with no limit on the intensity of enrollment or the type of program	For any year of undergraduate or graduate enrollment with no limit on the intensity of enrollment or the type of program
Effective date	Permanent program	Permanent program	Expires on January 1, 2006

FUNCTION - INTENDED BENEFICIARIES AND BENEFIT SIZE

Overview

Higher education tax benefits like other forms of federal financial aid are human capital investments expected to yield benefits for society and individual recipients. The tax benefits are not available to everyone seeking to meet postsecondary education expenses; rather they are primarily focused on specific groups of individuals and provide them with different amounts of assistance.

The tax benefits were enacted to help preserve and enhance access to postsecondary education for students from middle and upper middle income families. This group of families is not centrally targeted by most other federal aid programs, which place primary emphasis on assisting students with the greatest amount of financial need. Yet, middle income families make up a large proportion of the college population and face the challenge of meeting costs of higher education that have been increasing at a rate that has consistently outpaced inflation in recent decades.

Available data on tax benefit recipients indicate that the tax credits are, as intended, primarily serving middle and upper-middle income individuals. Preliminary data on the tax credits for tax year 1999 (see **Table 2**, below) reveal that over 39% of the 1999 tax returns claiming the education credits were from tax filers with adjusted gross income of $50,000 or more. These tax filers claimed nearly 46% of the total amount claimed in these credits for that year. In contrast, only about 11% of the returns claiming the credits were from tax filers with adjusted gross income of less than $15,000; these returns claimed less than 7% of total amount claimed.[17]

---

[17] The higher education deduction is not in effect yet, and thus no data can be provided on its claimants. It is similar to the Hope and Lifetime credits in that it targets middle income recipients. However, it phases out at higher income levels than the credits.

Table 2. Education Tax Credits, 1999 (Preliminary Data)

		Adjusted Gross Income			
	All Returns	Under $15,000	$15,000 under $30,000	$30,000 under $50,000	$50,000 under $100,000
Number of returns claiming credit	6,483,703	719,442	1,522,542	1,693,912	2,547,807
Percent of all returns claiming credit	100%	11%	23%	26%	39%
Amount of credit claimed ($ in thousands)	4,819,032	314,531	1,088,536	1,205,026	2,210,937
Percent of total claimed	100%	7%	23%	25%	46%

Source: IRS. Individual Income Tax Returns, Table 1. Sum of percentages may not equal 100% due to rounding. These data do not distinguish between the Hope and Lifetime Learning credits.

Intended Role for Each Benefit

The Hope and Lifetime credits were introduced together in 1997, as complementary benefits. The higher education tax deduction, introduced in 2001, extends their reach. In simplest terms the role envisioned for each benefit can be characterized in the following manner:

- The Hope credit was introduced to help ensure middle income students have universal access to the first 2 years of postsecondary education.

- The Lifetime Learning credit was designed to offer continued support to such traditional undergraduate students, not limited to the first 2 years of study. It also offers support to graduate students and "lifetime learners" (i.e., those not necessarily pursuing degrees).

- The higher education tax deduction will support the same set of higher educational pursuits as the Lifetime Learning credit, extending tax benefits to higher income individuals than either credit.

A more detailed discussion of these roles follows.

The Hope credit is targeted to a narrower group of postsecondary students — those in the first 2 years of postsecondary study, and enrolled half time or more in pursuit of a degree, certificate, or credential — than either the Lifetime Learning credit or the higher education deduction. For those individuals eligible for the Hope credit, it is likely to offer a more substantial benefit than either the Lifetime Learning credit or the new tax deduction. Beyond their first 2 years of postsecondary education, individuals enrolled on a halftone or more basis will benefit from either the lifetime Learning credit or the new tax deduction.

Significantly, the Lifetime Learning credit, which can be claimed for an unlimited number of years, supports traditional and nontraditional students regardless of their enrollment or degree status. Part-time and full time students can qualify for this credit as can graduate, undergraduate and non-degree students. These same eligibility criteria apply to the tax deduction. As a consequence, the Lifetime credit and the tax deduction occupy a unique niche in the student aid landscape. The Lifetime Learning credit currently, and the tax deduction prospectively, are widely available benefits that can support students who are taking occasional courses but are not necessarily enrolled in an educational credential or degree program. These may be a major source of direct financial aid available to many individuals who may want to take courses periodically over the course of their careers to upgrade their skills.[18]

Even though the Lifetime credit has been designed to provide aid to a wide array of students, it is likely that the credit will provide a good deal more benefit to traditional undergraduate and graduate students on *a per year basis* than to sporadic course-takers (e.g., those who may want to take courses periodically over the course of their careers to upgrade their skills). This is due to the fact that the credit covers 20% of higher education costs and traditional students are likely to incur more costs. However, sporadic course-takers can receive support for an unlimited number of years, and may ultimately gain more value from the credit *over a series of years* than do more traditional students. In much the same way, the tax deduction covers a broader array of courses of study and types of students but will deliver it greatest tax savings when the maximum qualified expenses are incurred, unlikely for taxpayers taking individual courses periodically.

---

[18] Among other more narrowly targeted benefits for individuals seeking to upgrade skills is employer education assistance.

Relative Worth of Each Benefit to Beneficiaries

The tax benefits were not designed to have seamless boundaries. In many instances their target populations overlap. Since many students are eligible for more than one of the benefits, taxpayers have to choose the appropriate benefit to realize the maximum value of assistance available to them. In general, when examining the relative worth of the benefits the following rules of thumb apply.

- As income increases, the thresholds at which the tax credits and tax deduction are eliminated become increasingly important in determining who can receive which benefit. The tax deduction's thresholds are higher than those for the Hope and Lifetime Learning credits.

- For those middle income taxpayers eligible to receive the Hope credit and whose incomes are under the phase out thresholds, the Hope credit is generally designed to be more valuable than either the Lifetime Learning credit or the tax deduction.

- For those middle income taxpayers eligible to receive the Lifetime but not the Hope credit and whose incomes are below the phase out thresholds, the relative value of the Lifetime Learning credit or the higher education deduction will depend on the taxpayers' marginal tax rate and qualified expenses.

A simple example illustrates that the Hope credit provides its beneficiaries with a potentially more substantial tax benefit than either of the other provisions. For an individual with $3,000 in qualified expenses in 2001 and whose modified adjusted gross income is below the beginning of the phase out thresholds, the Hope credit is worth a maximum of $1,500 (this is the overall maximum Hope credit reached when qualified expenses meet or exceed $2,000).[19] For that same individual with $3,000 in qualified expenses in 2001, the Lifetime Learning credit is worth a maximum of $600.[20] The Lifetime Learning credit's peak value for 2001 is $1,000, available when qualified expenses reach $5,000. The new tax deduction would be worth less

---

[19] The calculation is as follows: 100% of first $1,000 in qualified expenses = $1,000; 50% of the second $1,000 = $500.
[20] The calculation is as follows: 20% of $3,000 = $600.

to this individual than the Hope credit regardless of his or her marginal tax rate.

A more complex relationship exists between the tax deduction and Lifetime Learning credit. Basically, the relative worth of these benefits will likely hinge upon an individual's marginal tax rate. Depending upon the marginal tax rate, the deduction may be worth more or less than the Lifetime Learning credit. For example, a taxpayer with $3,000 in qualified higher education expenses would be better off taking the tax deduction than the Lifetime Learning credit if his or her marginal tax rate were 27% (deduction would be worth a maximum of $810 in reduced tax liability; Lifetime Learning credit would be worth a maximum of $600); but with a marginal tax rate of 15%, the Lifetime Learning credit would be worth more than the deduction (Lifetime Learning credit of $600 and a deduction reducing tax liability by $450).

Factors That Determine Benefit Size and Eligibility

The very structure of the Hope and Lifetime Learning credits and the higher education deduction dictates their focus on enhancing postsecondary access for students from middle and upper middle income families. What follows is a discussion of the mechanisms designed to "enforce" targeting and determine benefit value.

Eligibility and benefit size are a function of several key aspects of the tax credits and deduction. For example, as delineated above, intensity and level of enrollment can determine whether one is eligible for a Hope credit (available only to individuals enrolled at least half-time in their first 2 years of undergraduate education). The subsections below explore two additional sets of factors that play central roles in determining who is eligible for one of these benefits and how much the benefit will be:

- income and tax liability, and

- qualified tuition and related expenses.

Income and Tax Liability

As has already been shown, the Hope and Lifetime credits benefit middle income families. The income-related eligibility boundaries are established by income ceilings, and tax liability levels essentially function as a floor for the benefit.

The credits are fully phased out for taxpayers with modified adjusted gross income of over $50,000 ($100,000 in the case of a joint return). Filers earning more than those levels are ineligible for the credits.[21] The deduction extends federal tax benefits for postsecondary education expenses to higher income taxpayers.[22] For 2002 or 2003, the income threshold is $65,000 ($130,000 for joint returns). In 2004 or 2005, that threshold is raised still further so that filers with modified adjusted gross income of between $65,000 and $80,000 ($130,000 and $160,000 for joint filers) are eligible for the smaller deduction.

The credits only provide assistance to those with sufficient tax liability to claim nonrefundable credits. If there is no liability because a filer's income is completely offset by standard deductions and personal or dependent exemptions, neither credit may be claimed.[23] If the tax liability is below the maximum value of the credit, only the lesser amount may be claimed. Another factor that can affect the value of tax credits is the number of "competing credits" claimed by a tax filer. If a tax filer with limited tax liability claims competing tax credits such as dependent care tax credits, the full value of a Hope or Lifetime credit may not be realized because the other credits reduce the filer's liability below the amount of the education credits. For instance, if a tax filer has $1,000 in tax liability and qualifies for a $480 dependent care tax credit, $1,500 Hope credit for one student, and a $1,000 Lifetime credit for another student, the filer can only receive a total tax benefit of $1,000 (i.e., tax liability is less than the aggregate of credits for which the taxpayer may be eligible).

In contrast to the credits which reduce an individual's tax liability on a dollar for dollar basis, the deduction reduces a taxpayer's adjusted gross income. As was delineated in the example presented above, the potential impact of that reduction on tax liability is realized through the taxpayer's

---

[21] A high income family with a student for whom the dependent exemption could be claimed might decide not to make such a claim. This would allow the student to claim a credit assuming he or she has income below the phase out thresholds and has tax liability against which a credit could be taken.

[22] Although the income thresholds for the Hope and Lifetime Learning credits will be indexed for inflation after the 2001 tax year, the thresholds for the higher education tax deduction will still be significantly higher.

[23] The point at which a taxpayer will begin to have tax liability depends upon such factors as the taxpayer's income, number of dependents, and tax deductions. For example, a family of a husband and wife with a child in college, taking the standard deduction, would have no 2000 tax liability at an adjusted gross income level at or below $15,750, assuming this

marginal tax rate. Further, some taxpayers may have such limited tax liability *before* the application of the deduction that its actual benefit will be small.

Also, taxpayers seeking to claim the tax credits may be affected by the alternative minimum tax provisions that limit the aggregate nonrefundable personal credits a taxpayer can claim. As a result, some of these taxpayers may find the deduction to be a preferable option.

Qualified Tuition and Related Expenses

Students attending postsecondary education institutions where the qualified higher education expenses are less than the maximum allowable tax benefits will not be able to claim their full benefits. At many public institutions, low tuition and fee levels are likely to limit the ability to realize the full tax benefits. For the Hope tax credit, qualified higher education expenses must be at least $2,000 for the maximum credit to be realized. In academic year 1999-2000, average tuition and fees at public 2-year institutions were below that level ($1,705).[24] Realizing the full value of the Lifetime credit may be difficult for many students at public institutions in general — qualified expenses have to be at least $5,000 to actualize a $1,000 Lifetime Learning credit, markedly higher than the average tuition and fees at public 2-year or 4-year ($3,510) institutions. For the deduction, a taxpayer can claim the maximum deduction only if qualified expenses are $3,000 in 2002 and 2003, or $4,000 in 2004 and 2005. At $3,000, the average public 2-year tuition and fees are less; at $4,000, the average tuition and fees are less at both public 2-year and 4-year institutions.

In contrast, average tuition and fees at private institutions far exceeded any of the tax benefit maximums ($7,458 at 2-year private institutions, $16,332 at 4-year private institutions). Tuition and fees are probably sufficiently high at many of these institutions to pose no barrier on their own to realization of the full value of these credits and deduction.

The ability to capture the full value of these tax benefits is further limited by the fact that the Hope and Lifetime credits and the higher education tax deduction can be claimed to reimburse students and their families only for the *net* cost of qualified expenses, that is, the qualified expenses remaining after any non-taxable educational assistance received

---

family takes three exemptions of $2,800 apiece for a total of $8,400 and takes the standard deduction of $7,350.

[24] The College Board. *Trends in College Pricing 2000.* 2000.

(exclusive of loans and gifts) is subtracted. This reduces if not eliminates the tax benefits for many students receiving relatively large amounts of grant or scholarship aid. This is particularly the case for students receiving relatively large federal Pell Grant awards. Pell Grants are need-based grants that currently (2001-2002 award year) provide a maximum of $3,750 to the neediest students (i.e., students whose families are expected to contribute no resources toward postsecondary education costs). Students attending institutions with low tuition and fee charges and receiving large Pell Grants may have little or no net qualified expenses remaining for which to claim a credit or deduction. At the same time, these low-income students and their families may not have much if any tax liability, also restricting their ability to benefit from the credits or deduction.

As a result, students attending higher cost institutions, and those receiving relatively little grant or scholarship aid, are well positioned to capture a good deal of the potential value of their Hope and Lifetime credits and higher education deduction, assuming their families have sufficient tax liability to realize the maximum benefit from the credits or deduction.

RELATIONSHIP TO THE TRADITIONAL STUDENT AID DELIVERY SYSTEM

The introduction of the higher education tax benefits represented a departure from the federal government's more common practice of primarily making aid available through the traditional student aid delivery system. Given that the federal government is the primary provider of direct aid to students, and tax benefits have quickly grown to become a major component of the federal aid effort, considerable discussion has emerged related to the merits of providing aid through the tax system.

Providing student financial support toward meeting the costs of college through the federal income tax system has a number of advantages and disadvantages relative to the traditional process of providing grants, loans, and work support. Relevant issues are explored below.

Timing of Awards

One issue that distinguishes the traditional student aid system and the tax system is the timing of the awards. The traditional system provides aid such as grants and loans just in advance of the arrival of tuition bills. Tax credits and deductions, in contrast, require families to make an initial capital outlay which is reimbursed in the form of tax refunds arriving near the end of or after an academic year. This difference may limit the attractiveness of the tax system, particularly for lower income students who may not be able to meet current expenses that will be partly or fully reimbursed by a later tax benefit. Nevertheless, it is possible for taxpayers to adjust their tax withholding throughout the year in order to realize the tax benefits earlier. This would require some sophistication on the part of taxpayers. Further, for students enrolling in consecutive years, the tax benefit for a previous year may be provided in time to help meet the upcoming year's educational expenses. Finally, to the extent that the current tax benefits are available primarily to middle and upper middle income individuals, the timing issue may be less important.

Disbursement of Aid

Tax credits and deductions may offer the advantage of streamlined delivery of funds to aid recipients who directly claim their financial assistance as part of their annual tax-filing process. Most other aid is delivered through relatively cumbersome and labor intensive processes that require considerable effort on the part of financial aid officers, ED personnel, and loan servicers, in the case of loans, who must collectively certify student eligibility for aid, monitor enrollment status, disburse funds, and deal with refunds and account reconciliation.

Still, some have criticized the complexity of the process for taxpayers seeking to claim the tax benefits.[25] Further, there are institutional reporting requirements associated with the tax provisions that are viewed by some in the higher education community as potentially burdensome and expensive. TRA, as interpreted by the IRS, requires educational institutions to report to the IRS a broad array of data for any individual enrolled for academic credit for whom the institution receives tuition and fee payments. Of particular concern has been the requirement for institutions to report to the IRS for each student: the aggregate amounts of qualified expenses paid, scholarship and grant aid received, aggregate refunds made, and the identity of the taxpayer claiming the student as a tax dependent. The IRS limited the reporting requirements during the first four years of implementation (1998-

---

[25] See, for example, Wolanin, Thomas R. *Rhetoric and Reality: Effects and Consequences of the HOPE Scholarship.* The Institute for Higher Education Policy, April 2001. (Hereafter cited as Wolanin, *Rhetoric and Reality.*)

2001) to less than those stipulated by the TRA, Even these more limited reporting requirements have been criticized as costing institutions substantial resources.[26] P.L. 107-131 (signed into law on January 16, 2002) modifies some of the reporting requirements. Among other changes, it repeals the requirement regarding reporting of information about taxpayers who can claim students as dependents, and permits reporting of either the aggregate amounts of qualified expenses *paid* or the aggregate amounts *billed* to students.

Overall Complexity of College Financing

Given the extensive system already in place, the addition of the tax benefits, albeit delivered through an arguably more streamlined process, may actually increase the complexity of the overall national effort to help students and their families meet college costs. With the availability of the tax credits and the establishment of a new deduction, students and their families seeking to realize as much federally financed support as possible for college expenses must navigate not only the traditional financial aid system but also the federal income tax system. Potentially, the tax benefits may more likely be claimed successfully by sophisticated filers.

Direct Effect of Tax Benefits on Traditional Student Aid

The potential for a direct effect of these tax benefits on traditional student aid differs substantially between federal aid and non-federal aid.

Effect on Federal Student Aid

By statute, the receipt of the tax credits is to have *no effect* on a student's eligibility for, or level of federal student aid. First, in calculating what a student and his or her family is expected to contribute toward college costs (expected family contribution or EFC) under the Higher Education Act (HEA) student aid programs, HEA Section 480(a)(2) states that the tax

---

[26] Opposed IRS regulations issued June 16, 2000 (according to Internal Revenue Service Notice 2000-62, these regulations are to be finalized in 2001) would implement most, but not all, of the reporting requirements in TRA, applicable to returns required to be provided after December 31,2001. It would require reporting on the aggregate amounts paid, reimbursed or refunded, and received as grants or scholarships. Still, it would not require institutions to report the name, address, and taxpayer identification number of taxpayers claiming students as dependents for federal income tax purposes.

credits cannot be considered income or assets for purposes of that calculation. Second, HEA Section 480(a)(3) provides that the determination of need for HEA Title IV aid programs—student's cost of attendance minus the EFC and non-Title IV assistance — is not to include the credits as non-Title IV assistance. Any non-Title IV assistance included in this calculation reduces a student's need and, hence, his or her eligibility and level of assistance under need-based Title IV aid. There is no comparable language in the HEA governing the interaction between the new tax deduction and the Title IV assistance.

Tax benefits and Title IV aid may interact, however, in the federal funding process. It is possible that, in congressional deliberations over the budget and spending for federal programs, the forgone tax revenue associated with the tax benefit provisions may have a negative impact on the willingness or ability of the Congress to devote funds to the traditional federal student aid programs.

Effect on Packaging of Other Aid

The limited evidence available suggests that financial aid officers are far from uniform in whether or how they consider the tax benefits when packaging financial aid for students. Indeed, it is not clear whether the majority actively factors the tax benefits into this process at all.

Financial aid officers who want to factor the tax credits into their aid packaging calculations may find the effort complicated by the absence of information about the actual value of the tax benefits students will receive. As noted earlier, tax benefits are claimed and their value known by April 15 of the year after the payment for qualified expenses are made.

Certain other aspects of the design of the tax benefits may make it difficult to infer their value before they are claimed. The actual value of the tax benefits to recipients is affected by a series of offsets and limitations that are built into the design of the tax system (for example, as explored earlier, a recipient must have sufficient tax liability to claim the credit and even then the value of the credit may be reduced by competing credits that can be claimed). The potential effects of these internal offsets and limitations make it hard for financial aid officers to project the value of the credit when packaging aid.

Those financial aid officers who would take the tax provisions into account in packaging aid, and thereby, reduce other kinds of aid for recipients, must make assumptions about the benefits' value. If gaps exist

Effect on State Decisions Related to Tuition Levels and Available Sources of Aid

between the credits' actual and assumed value the recipients may receive more or less aid than intended.

The effect of the tax benefits on the setting of tuition levels by states is largely unknown. State higher education officials face challenges similar to those faced by financial aid officers stemming from the hidden value of tax credits. They must make decisions about tuition levels at state institutions and about the structure and targeting of state aid programs which can be shaped in part by assumptions about the value of aid that they expect will be available to students. Precisely gauging the net financial benefit flowing from the tax benefits is problematic, however some states have considered, at least, raising the tuition and fees in some schools in order to enable their students to "capture" as much of the tax benefits as possible. Some states have also considered targeting their state grant programs in ways that avoid inhibiting students' ability to capture the full value of other credits.[27] Such decisions regarding tuition and aid will affect whether and how the tax benefits will enhance recipients' ability to finance postsecondary education.

---

[27] One recent analysis that has explored available information on this issue concludes that the Hope Scholarship provides resources that "are an incentive for private and public institutions of higher education to increase tuition or to reduce aid to students. Indeed, the HOPE Scholarship benefits institutions of higher education *only if* they raise tuition or decrease student aid. Several states have considered or undertaken strategies to capture the HOPE Scholarship through either tuition increases or aid reduction." (Wolanin, *Rhetoric and Reality*, p. 29)

Chapter 2

HIGHER EDUCATION TAX CREDITS: TARGETING VALUE, AND INTERACTION WITH OTHER FEDERAL STUDENT AID

SUMMARY

The Taxpayer Relief Act of 1997 (P.L. 105-34) authorized two new tax credits for family postsecondary education expenses. The Hope Scholarship Credit provides up to 1,500 in annual tax relief to defray the cost of the first 2 years of undergraduate studies. The Lifetime Learning Credit provides up to 1,000 in tax relief to defray the cost of any year to help preserve and enhance access to postsecondary study. The Hope and Lifetime Learning Credits were enacted to help preserve and enhance access to postsecondary education for students from middle-income families.

There are no national data provide the comprehensive information needed to thoroughly analyze the distribution of the education tax credits and their interaction with traditional student aid awarded under the Higher Education Act (HEA). This chapter examines these issues by using two different modeling approaches to estimate the benefits potentially offered by the credits to young adults who are currently out-of-school, and the eligibility of currently enrolled aided students for the tax benefits and how much they might receive. Modeling is also used to estimate changes in the targeting of federal "obligation-free" aid (grants and tax credits), and the distributional effects of changes to the credits.

The results from this analysis are legislatively relevant because the 107th Congress is considering proposals to change the size and targeting of the education credits. Further, the interaction of the credits and HEA student aid will likely be of legislative interest during 108th Congress when the HEA is up for reauthorization.

Briefly, the major findings from this analysis are as follows.

The Hope Credit provides a substantial benefit to recipients and spreads these benefits relatively broadly. By design, these credits target the bulk of their benefits to middle and upper-middle-income students. But, these benefits also reach down to some low-income students, overlapping with the major source of federal grant aid – Pell Grants.

The Lifetime Learning Credit, in contrast, provides relatively little benefit. Students attending higher priced institutions are much more likely to maximize the amount of Lifetime Learning Credit they receive.

The Hope and Lifetime Learning Credits have tended to shift the focus of federal postsecondary obligation-free aid. Such aid is no longer principally need-based aid targeted to the lowest income students, but is now available to the broad expanse of middle and upper middle-income student.

There is current congressional interest in modifying the distribution of the tax credit benefits. The current patterns of distribution are a function of often complex interaction among the credits' award rules. For instance, to extend tax credit benefits to low-income students at lower priced institutions concurrent changes to several of the award rules may be required.

INTRODUCTION

The Taxpayer Relief Act of 1997 (P.L 105-34) authorized two new tax credits for family postsecondary education expenses. The Hope Scholarship Credit provides up to $1,500 in annual tax relief to defray the cost of the first 2 years of undergraduate studies. The Lifetime Learning Credit provides up to $1,000 in tax relief to defray the cost of any year of postsecondary study.[1] The Hope and Lifetime Learning Credits were enacted to help preserve and enhance access to postsecondary education for students from middle-income families.

Since being introduced, the tax credits have rapidly become major sources of assistance for postsecondary students nationwide. They have also added considerable complexity to the student aid picture largely because it has been difficult to assemble precise information about the population of

---

[1] For a detailed discussion of the features of the Hope Credit and Lifetime Learning Credit, see CRS Report RL31129, Higher Education Tax Credits and Deduction: An Overview of the Benefits and Their Relationship to Traditional Student Aid, by Adam Stoll and James Stedman.

students receiving each credit, and about how the credits interact with other forms of aid.

There are no national data that provide the comprehensive information needed to address the issues of the distribution of the education tax credits and their interaction with other forms of aid. The tax credits operate outside of the systems used for packaging and awarding student financial aid. Consequently, information on the receipt of tax credits is not available in the large-scale national surveys on aid received by students — which are reliant on institutional reporting of aid packages "awarded" to students. Additionally, available data from the Internal Revenue Service (IRS) have serious limitations and are not well suited for use in examining the tax credit benefits received in particular academic years, or for making comparisons between those benefits and other financial aid.

Adding to this challenge, tax credit values cannot be easily inferred. The actual value of the credits is often less than the maximum possible value, due in large part to a series of offsets and limitations built into the design of the credits.[2]

Despite the growing importance of tax credits, higher education analysts and policymakers have had a difficult time assessing the value of the credits for varied groups of recipients, and pinpointing how the credits interact with other forms of aid. These are important issues to resolve because there currently are a number of proposals under consideration in the 107th Congress that would affect the size and targeting of the Hope and Lifetime Learning Credits. Additionally, the interaction between tax credits and other forms of federal student aid will likely be of particular legislative interest during the 108th Congress when the Higher Education Act will next be up for reauthorization.

In an effort to add clarity to this situation, this chapter presents newly generated estimates of the value of the credits available to varied eligible recipients. In the absence of actual data, modeling approaches that simulate tax credit values offer perhaps the most promising way to examine the targeting of the education tax credits. Two different modeling approaches are applied in the analysis presented in this chapter. These models, described later, are used to provide the following:

- the estimated benefits potentially offered by the credits to young adults who are currently out of school;

---

[2] These offsets and limitations are considered in detail below.

- estimated eligibility of currently enrolled aided students for the tax benefits;
- estimates of changes in the targeting of federal obligation-free aid (discussed later in this chapter); and
- estimates of the effects of possible changes in the award rules of the credits on expanding the distribution of the benefits to lower income students, thereby, potentially increasing their impact on access.

The Hope and Lifetime Learning Credits are premised on the assumption that tax benefits reaching a maximum of between $1,000 and $1,500 will enhance access to postsecondary education. This analysis delineates how these benefits might be distributed to current and potential student populations for whom access is likely to be an important issue. Nevertheless, it is beyond the scope of the present chapter to determine whether tax benefits of these amounts will, in fact, expand access to postsecondary education for these populations.

Analytic Approaches to Examining the Value of Tax Credits

The Hope and Lifetime Learning Credits were intended to enhance or help preserve college access.[3] In keeping with the aims of the credits, this examination will focus on the level of assistance they can provide to populations for whom access may be an issue.

Populations Being Analyzed

The first group is the broad population of college-age individuals who, although they have graduated from high school, are not currently participating in postsecondary education. It is considered to be comprised of "potential postsecondary education students." The second group is the population of postsecondary students who are currently receiving federal financial assistance to help support their studies. This group includes the preponderance of higher education students receiving need-based aid.

---

[3] The Clinton Administration first proposed the Hope Credits in 1997 in order to "provide tax relief to middle-income families struggling to pay for college" and to "help make 14 years of education the standard for all Americans." (Letter dated March 20,1997 to Speaker of the House Newt Gingrich from Secretary of Education Richard W. Riley and Secretary of the Treasury Robert Rubin.)

Students enrolled in postsecondary education, but not receiving financial aid, are not being studied since access is not dependent on federal financial aid for this population.

Analytical Approach — Case Simulation Modeling[4]

The initial analysis focuses on the broad population of potential postsecondary students who are not currently enrolled in postsecondary education, and uses a case simulation model. Case simulations are used to explore how the following factors affect the tax credit levels: income, offsets, family composition, cost of education, and type of institution attended. This examination explores what the tax credits might really be worth to different kinds of prospective students.

We explore these issues by first analyzing Current Population Survey (CPS) data from the Bureau of the Census to construct a set of cases that typify characteristics of the current potential postsecondary student population. These cases were then run through the model to determine the level of tax credit assistance likely to flow to them. A sufficient number of cases were run to map thresholds, cut-off points, gaps in coverage, and to thoroughly explore issues related to offsets.

Analytical Approach — Survey Data Modeling[5]

The second approach focuses on aided enrolled postsecondary students. This analysis utilizes the National Postsecondary Student Aid Study (NPSAS) data on students' tax liability, income, attendance status, enrollment status, grant aid, and tuition and fee levels to construct estimated tax credit values for students receiving financial aid. NPSAS provides comprehensive nationally representative data on the financial aid packages received by students. Under this approach, once estimated tax credit values are computed for students, it is possible to examine the level of tax credit benefits potentially available to students possessing different characteristics, and how the tax credits complement other sources of aid in helping students meet tuition costs.

---

[4] For additional information, see the technical appendix to this chapter.
[5] Ibid.

WHAT BENEFITS DO THE CREDITS OFFER PROSPECTIVE STUDENTS?

This section of the chapter considers the estimated distribution for 2001-2002 of the tax credit benefits, as well as Pell Grant aid, to out-of-school young adults who have at least graduated from high school but who have not attained a bachelor's degree (BA).[6] This is a population which, if it enrolled in postsecondary education, could be eligible for the tax credits and Pell Grants. The Pell Grant program is the largest federal grant program for postsecondary undergraduates, providing some $9.9 billion in grant aid for the 2001-2002 academic year and $10.7 billion for 2002-2003. As is delineated below, Pell Grant aid has a critical impact on the distribution of the education tax credits.

As noted earlier, this portion of the chapter utilizes a case simulation model which shows how the distribution of tax credit benefits and Pell Grant assistance changes as adjusted gross income (AGI) changes. The results generated by this case simulation model are linked to the young out-of-school population through an analysis of data gathered by the Bureau of the Census' CPS for March 2000.[7] Analysis of CPS data identified primary groups within the pool of young out-of-school prospective students. The distribution of aid to two of the primary groups of prospective students is considered throughout the remainder of this section:

- young out-of-school married individuals who are at least high school graduates but who have not earned a BA, and who are independent for need analysis purposes[8] and federal income tax purposes; and

---

[6] These individuals may have never attended postsecondary education or may have some postsecondary enrollment without attaining a degree higher than an associate's degree.

[7] The March CPS is a survey of approximately 50,000 households, collecting detailed data on labor force participation and income. Information on current educational activity is collected for individuals aged 16 to 24. The March 2000 survey was used to estimate the characteristics of the portion of this young population who were high school graduates, not currently enrolled in college, and had not earned a BA (if they had enrolled in college previously).

[8] "For federal student aid, an individual is considered independent of his or her parents (i.e., parental income and assets are not considered in determining the assistance), if the individual is at least 24 years old by December 31 of the award year, is an orphan or ward of the state (or was until age 18), is a veteran of the armed forces, is a graduate or professional student, is married, has dependents others than a spouse, or is deemed independent by a financial aid officer for "other unusual circumstances." To distinguish the financial aid dependents from independents in the CPS young out-of-school population, all of these factors were applied, except whether the individual was or had

- young single (no spouse or other dependent) out-of-school independents with the same educational attainment as the first group.[9]

Quintile distributions of the AGI of the target subgroups of this young out-of-school population are mapped to the case simulation results to show what the potential benefits are for different income quintiles.[10]

Summary of Findings

Briefly, the findings presented in this section include the following:

- The distribution of assistance reflects the basic design of the credits which, by virtue of their nonrefundability and grant aid offset (these features are discussed below), are targeted to students in the middle to upper middle income quintiles. The credits will not affect access for the lowest income students because they provide no benefit to such students.

- Nevertheless, the tax benefits, particularly the Hope Credits, may be received by some low-income students who also receive Pell Grants. This may boost federal aid to a portion of the low-income population.

- Under most circumstances, the Hope Credit appears to offer a much greater benefit than does the Lifetime Learning Credit. The size of a

---

been an orphan or ward of the state, and whether a financial aid officer might make a determination that the individual was financially independent.

[9] According to CPS data, an estimated 2.0 million individuals are in the first group (young out-of-school married independents); 65% of these individuals are high school graduates only, 35% have some college but not a BA An estimated 2.9 million individuals are in the second group (young out-of-school single independents); 62% are high school graduates only; 38% have some college but less than a BA A third group, whose benefits were analyzed, but for whom results are not displayed, are dependent young individuals living with two parents. There are approximately 660,000 individuals in this group (32% are high school graduates only; 68% have some college but less than a BA). The simulated distribution of Pell Grants and education tax credits to this third subgroup parallels to a substantial degree the results for the young married independent population.

[10] The AGI quintile breaks shown in the figures in this section are point estimates based on CPS survey data and are meant to be illustrative. Given sampling and nonsampling errors, actual quintiles for the populations analyzed might differ from those shown here. The March 2000 CPS survey provides estimates of 1999 AGI. These were inflated to 2001 using the CPI-U (a 6.3% increase).

Lifetime Learning Credit is generally insignificant relative to the absolute benefit derived from a Pell Grant or a Hope Credit, or relative to tuition and fees or the cost of attendance (for delineation of tuition and fees, and cost of attendance, see footnote 17).

Award Rules

The analysis of the distribution and value of the Hope and Lifetime Learning Credits in this and the following sections of the chapter depends, in part, on an understanding of how the credits are calculated for an individual. This involves an explanation of the award rules for the credits. As delineated below, a key rule concerns the interaction of the credits with other grant aid an individual might receive. The primary source of federal grant aid to undergraduates is the Pell Grant program. As a consequence, information on how Pell Grant aid is determined is also important for a fuller understanding of the operation of the education credits. This portion of the chapter provides an overview of the award rules for the Pell Grants and the education credits.

Pell Grants

In general, the amount of Pell Grant assistance an individual receives is the difference between the maximum Pell Grant being awarded in any particular year and the individual's expected family contribution (EFC).[11] For all simulated cases, this is the award rule applied. As the EFC rises (generally, as the family's AGI increases), the Pell Grant shrinks. Among the key features of the Pell Grant calculation most relevant for this analysis are that the grant is not affected by the receipt of other student financial aid, and that the poorest individuals (those with zero EFCs) receive the maximum Pell Grant ($3,750 for award year 2001-2002). Further, the Pell Grant assistance can cover all postsecondary education expenses (as noted below, the education tax credits currently can only cover qualified tuition and fee expenses).

Figure 1 below shows the estimated amount of Pell Grant assistance for award year 2001-2002 to which a married independent student with a child

---

[11] A student's EFC is based on consideration of his or her income and other financial resources, as well as those of a spouse (if married) or of parents (if considered dependent for need analysis). The amount of a student's Pell Grant is the least of the following three calculations: annual maximum Pell Grant minus EFC; cost of attendance minus EFC; or the tuition sensitivity rule (applicable only when tuition is very low). As noted in the text, for most students, the first calculation determines the size of the Pell Grant.

might be entitled based on AGI and other characteristics.[12] In this case, the student is a high school graduate who has never previously enrolled in college (a candidate for receipt of a Hope Credit). The Pell Grant aid is represented by the lightly shaded area. The thick vertical bars overlaid on the figure show the distribution of AGI by quintiles based on data for individuals with these characteristics (for this and all subsequent figures, the 4th and 5th quintiles are grouped together).

Figure 1. Pell Grant for 16-24 Year Old Married Independent High School Graduate (with a Child) Enrolling Full-time at a Community College

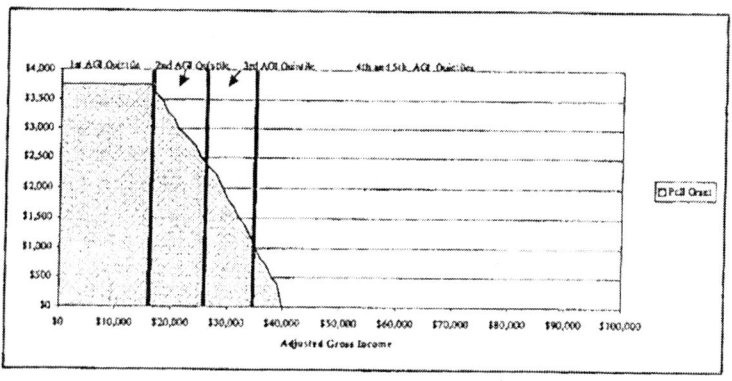

As shown in Figure 1, this type of student realizes the maximum Pell Grant when AGI is between $0 and an estimated $16,000. As AGI increases above $16,000 and EFC for the student begins to rise above $0, the amount of Pell Grant aid declines, until it reaches $0 when AGI is $40,000. Across the first quintile (i.e., the students falling into the lowest 20% of this group by AGI), the Pell Grant is at its maximum. In the 2nd quintile of AGI, the Pell Grant begins to decline.

Education Tax Credits

The Hope and Lifetime Learning Credits are *nonrefundable* tax credits, meaning they are available only to the extent that the taxpayer has income

---

[12] According to the March 2000 CPS data, the median family size of the young out-of-school independent with a spouse was 3. As a result, the case simulations of Pell Grant and Hope Credits were based on this family size.

tax liability. Further, they are applied against "qualified" higher education expenses. Qualified expenses are tuition and fees required as a condition for enrollment.[13] These expenses are reduced by the amount of non-taxable educational assistance received by the student, which includes Pell Grants. We call the reduction in qualified expenses the *grant aid offset*.

For individuals, both credits begin to be phased out after AGI exceeds $40,000 and are completely phased out when income reaches $50,000, For those who are married filing joint returns, these income thresholds are $80,000 and $100,000.[14]

The credits differ in several key ways. To be eligible for a Hope Credit, an individual must be enrolled on at least a half-time basis in a program leading to a degree, certificate, or credential; and he or she cannot have finished the first 2 years of undergraduate education. In contrast, the Lifetime Learning Credit is available for individuals enrolled in one or more courses of undergraduate or graduate instruction to acquire or improve job skills, and there is no limit on the number of years for which the credit may be claimed.

Perhaps most significantly, the reimbursement rules for qualified expenses differ between the two credits. For the 2001 tax year, the Hope Credit is equal to 100% of the first $1,000 in qualified expenses and 50% of the second $1,000 in qualified expenses, capped at a maximum credit of $1,500.[15] For that same year, the Lifetime Learning Credit is equal to 20% of the first $5,000 in qualified expenses, for a maximum credit of $1,000.[16]

Figure 2 shows the distribution of the Hope Credit to the same type of student as considered in Figure 1. Tax credit assistance is depicted by the darkly shaded area. The Hope Credit distribution has been adjusted, as necessary, by the Pell Grant assistance received (which is not shown in the figure).

---

[13] As noted below, the tuition and fees, and cost of attendance levels used for this analysis are annual averages determined by the College Board. It was assumed that the estimated average tuition and fees constituted qualified expenses for these case simulations. That is, all fees included in these estimates were assumed to be required as a condition for enrollment.

[14] The thresholds for phasing out the tax credits are based on modified AGI which for most taxpayers is equivalent to their AGI. No adjustment to AGI was made for these simulated cases. These various income thresholds for the phase-outs will be indexed to inflation beginning after tax year 2001.

[15] After tax year 2001, the maximum Hope Credit will be indexed for inflation.

[16] For qualified expenses paid after December 31, 2002, the credit will be a maximum of $2,000, calculated as 20% of the first $10,000 in qualified expenses.

Figure 2. Hope Credit for 16-24 Year Old Married Independent High School Graduate (with a Child) Enrolling Full-time at a Community College (Adjusted for Pell Grant Aid)

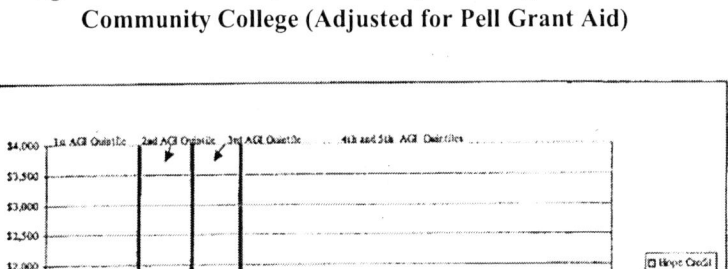

For this type of student, the Hope Credit can first be realized when AGI reaches approximately $31,000. The credit rises to $1,369, the maximum that this student can receive, when AGI reaches $40,000. This is not the full $1,500 ceiling for the Hope Credit because of the credit's reimbursement rules. In this case, the student is assumed to be enrolling at a community college where, on average for academic year 2001-2002, the tuition and fees are $1,738 (see footnote 17). The Hope Credit provides 100% reimbursement of the first $1,000 of this average tuition and fee level and 50% of the remainder (i.e., $738) or $369, for a maximum credit of $1,369 for this student. This type of student can receive this maximum Hope Credit until AGI reaches $80,000 where the credit's phase-out rule applies. At $100,000, the benefit is fully phased out.

The Hope Credit provides no benefit to the lowest 2 quintiles; provides some assistance in the 3rd quintile; and provides the maximum benefit across the 4th and 5th quintiles.

The aggregate Hope Credit and Pell Grant aid received by this type of student is shown in Figure 3. The top line that traces areas covered by the Pell Grant and the Hope Credit is the aggregate aid being realized by this type of student as AGI changes. In the zone where the credit and the grant overlap, the Hope Credit provides some modest compensation for the decline in Pell Grant aid.

Figure 3. Hope Credit and Pell Grant for 16-24 Year Old Married Independent High School Graduate (with a Child) Enrolling Full-time at a Community College

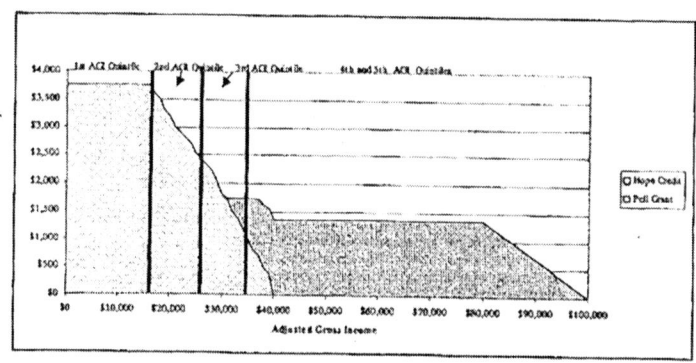

Who in the Young Out-of-School Population is Potentially Served by Hope Credits?

The analysis considers the differences in distribution of benefits across three categories of institutions in which most students are found—community college, 4-year public college, or 4-year private college; these institutional categories differ markedly with regard to average tuition and fees, and average cost of attendance.[17]

Married Independent Student With a Child Across Institutional Categories

Figure 3 above depicts the distribution of Pell Grant and Hope Credit assistance for this type of student enrolled at a community college. The next two figures show the benefits if the student attended a 4-year public college or a 4-year private college.

---

[17] The costs of attendance and tuition and fees for each type of institution are sample undergraduate budgets, derived from the College Board's Trends in College Pricing 2001. For community colleges, the average cost of attendance was $10,367 and average tuition and fees was $1,738; for 4-year public colleges, the respective averages were $11,976 and $3,754; for 4-year private colleges, the respective averages were $26,070 and $17,123. The cost of attendance includes not only estimates of the average tuition and fees, but also the average expenses for room and board, books and supplies, transportation, and other miscellaneous expenses. All tuition and fees are for in-state students.

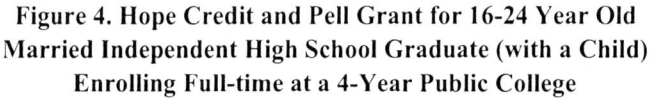

Figure 4. Hope Credit and Pell Grant for 16-24 Year Old Married Independent High School Graduate (with a Child) Enrolling Full-time at a 4-Year Public College

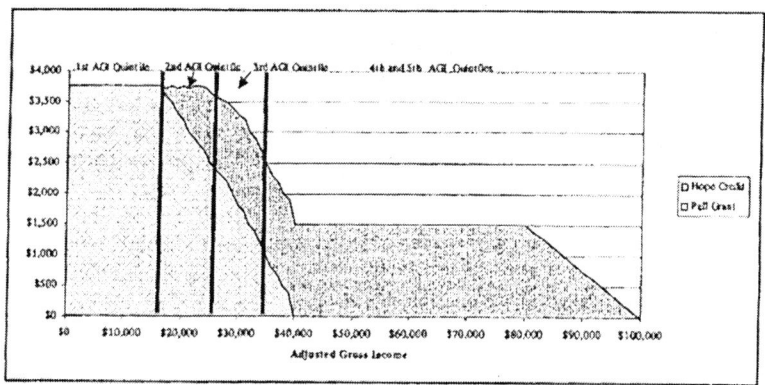

The key points that can be made about the distribution of benefits are the following:• The higher average tuition and fee levels of 4-year institutions compared to those at community colleges allow the maximum Hope Credit of $1,500 to be claimed.

- For each institutional category, there is a range of income across which both Pell Grant aid and Hope Credit benefit may be received. This income range is relatively narrow at the community college level ($31,000 to $39,000) because of its lower average tuition and fees.[18] In contrast, the income range where the benefits overlap is significantly wider at 4-year institutions ($ 17,000 to $39,000), primarily a function of the higher average tuition and fees.[19] As a result of these higher charges, the Hope Credit reaches down into the 2nd AGI quintile. Indeed, for this income quintile, the Hope

---

[18] The Pell Grant does not fall below $1,738 (the tuition and fees being paid) until AGI reaches $30,000; only at that juncture are there remaining qualified expenses that can be covered by the Hope Credit.

[19] The $17,000 starting point of this income range is where this type of student's EFC first exceeds $0. There are substantial qualified expenses remaining after the grant aid offset that can be covered by the Hope Credit at these institutions.

Credit effectively replaces Pell Grant assistance that was lost as AGI rose.[20]

- Coverage of average tuition and fees by the maximum Hope Credit that can be realized is highest at the community college level (79%) and drops precipitously at the 4-year public and 4-year private college levels (40% and 9%, respectively).[21]

Figure 5. Hope Credit and Pell Grant for 16-24 Year Old Married Independent High School Graduate (with a Child) Enrolling Full-time at a 4-Year Private College

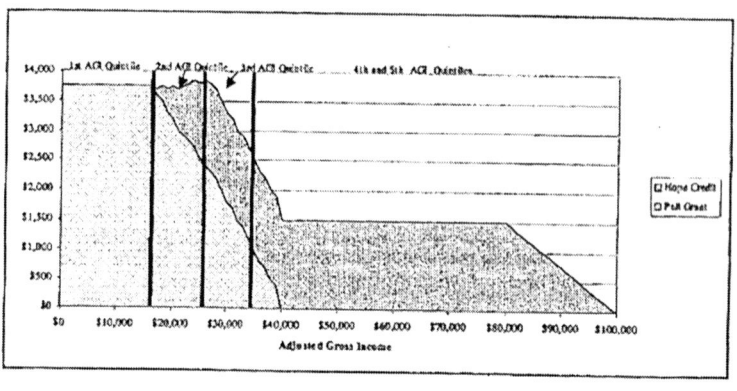

Single Independent Student Across Institutional Categories

The following figures show the distribution, across institutional categories, of Pell Grant and Hope Credit benefits for a single independent individual.[22] The 4-year public college and 4-year private college categories

---

[20] At some points in the 2nd AGI income quintile, the combination of Hope Credit and Pell Grant exceeds the maximum Pell Grant which students in the 1st income quintile receive. This is clearer in the figure showing benefits at the 4-year private college.

[21] Each of these percentages is calculated using the maximum credit that can be realized for each simulated case and the relevant average tuition and fees delineated in footnote 17.

[22] For these figures, the X-axis (adjusted gross income) extends only from $0 to $50,000 (not $100,000 as with the married independent student) because that is the range of income across which the Hope Credit can be claimed by this type of student who is ineligible to file a joint return.

are displayed in a single figure since the distribution of aid for this case is identical for these two categories of institution.[23]

Figure 6. Hope Credit and Pell Grant for 16-24 Year Old Single Independent High School Graduate Enrolling Full-time at a Community College

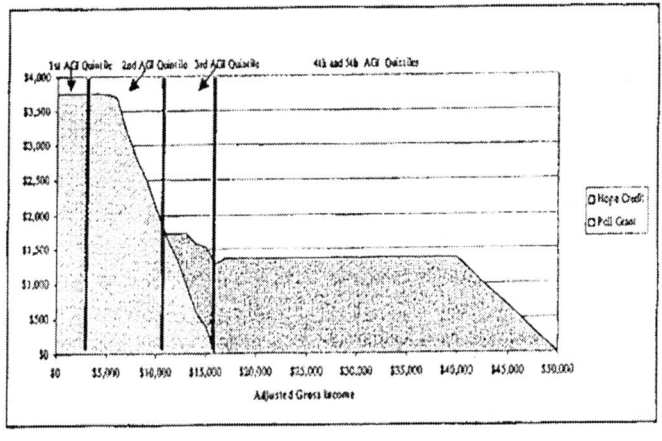

---

[23] The early loss of Pell Grant assistance and the nonrefundability of the Hope Credit explain why there is no difference between the distribution for these students in a 4-year public college and in a 4-year private college. As the Pell Grant is reduced, more tuition and fees remain to be covered by the credit. But, at and beyond the lower AGI where the Pell Grant phases out, it is tax liability that dictates how much credit can be claimed. Tax liability does not differ across categories of institutions. As a result, there is no difference in the benefits realized.

Figure 7. Hope Credit and Pell Grant for 16-24 Year Old Single Independent High School Graduate Enrolling Full-time at Either a 4-Year Public College or a 4-Year Private College

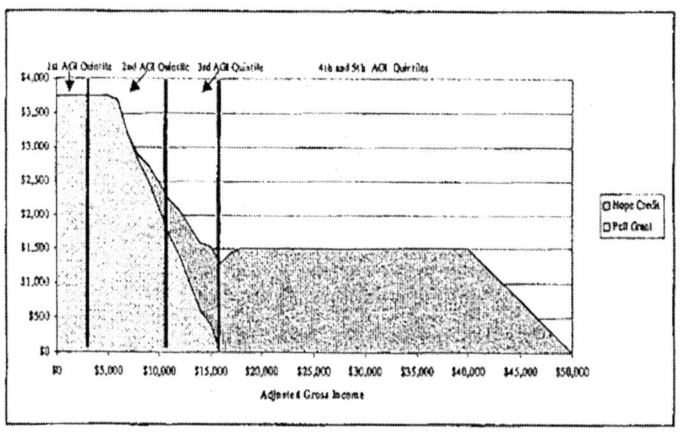

Analysis of these figures reveals that the distribution of Pell Grant and Hope Credit benefits to single independent students differs from that of married independent students. Among the important differences are the following:

- The maximum Pell Grant assistance is provided over a much narrower range of AGIs and declines to zero much sooner (at approximately $16,000 AGI versus $40,000 AGI for the married independent student case). This in turn permits the Hope Credit to be claimed lower down the income range because the rapid diminution of the Pell Grant aid frees up tuition and fees for potential coverage by the credit.[24]

- The income quintiles are more clustered at the lower end of the income scale than they are for the married independent student, somewhat changing the relative balance of grant aid and credit benefit in the income quintiles. The Hope Credit offers less

---

[24] "The dip in aggregate assistance at an income of approximately $16,000 is a function of a Pell award rule not considered previously—when a student's calculated Pell Grant falls in the $200 to $400 range, a $400 grant is awarded. This means there is a sudden decline from a $400 Pell Grant to $0 when the calculated Pell Grant is below $200. Where this

assistance in the 2nd and 3rd quintiles to the single independent student than to the married independent student.

- Coverage of average tuition and fees by the maximum Hope Credit that can be realized is the same for this type of student as for married independent students (see above).

Half-time Enrollment

When either of these student cases is enrolled on a half-time basis at a 4-year public or private college, Pell Grant assistance can be markedly reduced while the Hope Credit remains relatively unchanged. As a consequence, at these kinds of institutions, the amount of benefit provided by this tax credit may be closer to the size of the Pell Grant benefit.[25] In contrast, at community colleges, the Pell Grant and Hope Credit are both likely to be reduced, roughly proportionately.

WHO IN THE YOUNG OUT-OF-SCHOOL POPULATION IS POTENTIALLY SERVED BY LIFETIME LEARNING CREDITS?

In general, the Lifetime Learning Credit delivers markedly less benefit than does the Hope Credit This is primarily a function of the different reimbursement rules between the two credits. The maximum Hope Credit is 50% larger than the maximum Lifetime Learning Credit. Further, when tuition and fee levels that can be covered by the credits are relatively low, the Lifetime Learning Credit can be substantially less than the Hope Credit. For example, if remaining tuition and fees are $2,000, a $1,500 Hope Credit might be claimed given sufficient tax liability but the maximum Lifetime Learning Credit at that tuition and fee level is only $200.

---

occurs for these independent students, there is not sufficient tax liability for the Hope Credit to cover the marked increase in remaining tuition and fees.

[25] Under the Pell Grant program, the award for a half-time student is calculated based on a ratable reduction of the full-time award. In contrast, the Hope Credit was calculated by reducing the average tuition and fees for each category of institution by 50%. At lower priced institutions, such as community colleges, this reduces the allowable credit since initial tuition and fee levels are at or below the $2,000 tuition level at which the maximum Hope Credit can be claimed (given the credit's reimbursement rules). At higher priced institutions, tuition is sufficiently large that a 50% reduction need not affect the maximum Hope Credit benefit.

Married Independent Students with a Child Across Institutional Categories

The analysis below focuses on the distribution of Pell Grant and Lifetime Learning Credit benefits to a married independent student with a child. This individual has some college but has not earned a BA. This student is assumed to be a candidate for the Lifetime Learning Credit and not eligible for the Hope Credit.[26]

Figure 8. Lifetime Learning Credit and Pell Grant for 16-24 Year Old Married Independent (with a Child) Having Some College Enrolling Full-time at a Community College

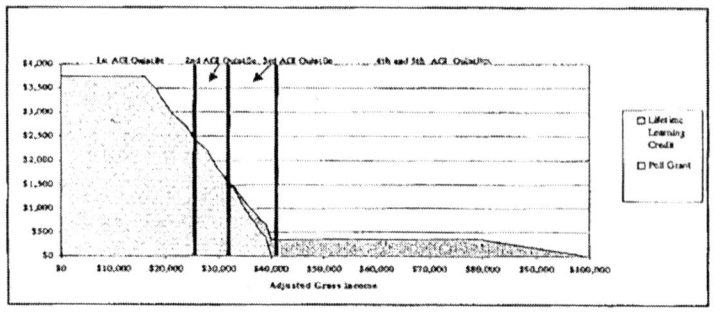

---

[26] In the March CPS, the educational attainment variable does not permit one to identify the specific number of years of attainment the out-of-school 16-24 year old might have the undergraduate categories are some college, AA (academic) degree, AA (vocational) degree, and BA. For this analysis, the first three categories were collapsed in order to identify the undergraduate who might be eligible for the Lifetime Learning Credit. Limiting educational attainment in this manner was dictated by the fact that almost without exception the Pell Grant is available only to undergraduates (i.e., individuals without a BA degree).

Higher Education Tax Credits: Targeting Value, and Interaction... 39

Figure 9. Lifetime Learning Credit and Pell Grant for 16-24 Year Old Married Independent (with a Child) Having Some College Enrolling Full-time at a 4-Year Public College

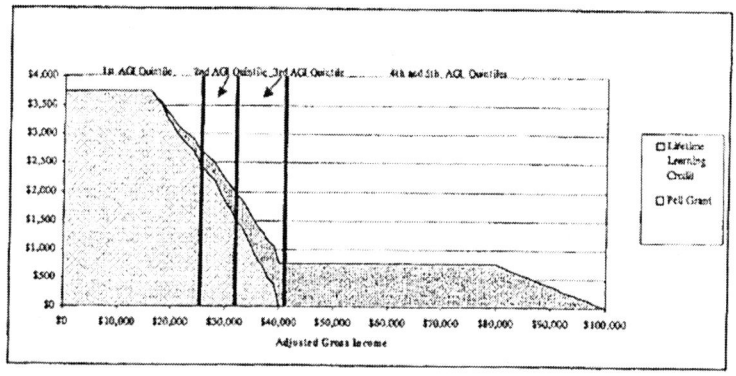

Figure 10. Lifetime Learning Credit and Pell Grant for 16-24 Year Old Married Independent (with a Child) Having Some College Enrolling Full-time at a 4-Year Private College

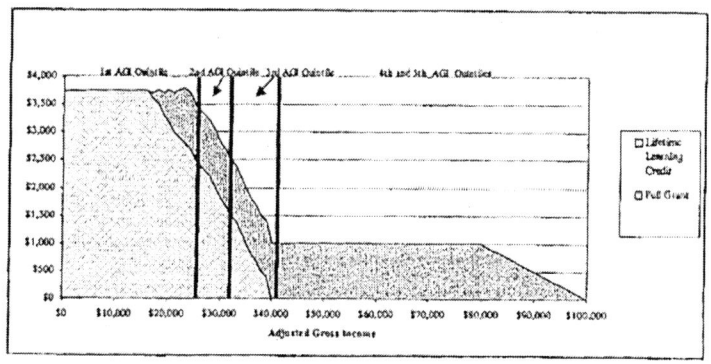

Several key points can be made about the simulated distribution of these benefits:

- The Lifetime Learning Credit is maximized when tuition levels are highest. The credit offers little absolute assistance to a student attending the community college or even the 4-year public college. It is only at the much higher tuition and fee levels at the 4-year private college that the maximum Lifetime Learning Credit can be claimed.

- The Lifetime Learning Credit reaches down into the 1st income quintile only at relatively high tuition levels. At the 4-year private college for this student, the credit more than offsets the loss of Pell Grant aid for the upper reaches of the 1st income quintile.

- The level of estimated Lifetime Learning Credit assistance received by these students is significantly less than the Hope Credit benefits received by the other subset of married independent students (those with only a high school diploma). The coverage of average tuition and fee charges by the maximum Lifetime Learning Credit that can be realized is markedly less — 20% at the community college (compared to 79% by the Hope Credit for the other subset of students), 20% at the 4-year public college (40% by the Hope Credit for the other subset), and 6% at the 4-year private college (9% by the Hope Credit for the other subset).[27]

Single Independent Students Across Institutional Categories

The figures below show the estimated distribution of benefits for a single independent student case where the individual has some college but less than a bachelor's degree (BA).

---

[27] Given that the average tuition and fees at the community college and 4-year public college are less than $5,000, the maximum coverage possible with the Lifetime Learning Credit under its reimbursement rules is 20%. At the much higher average tuition and fee levels at the 4-year private college ($17,123), the cap on the maximum Lifetime Learning Credit ($1,000) sharply reduces the percentage coverage of tuition and fees ($1,000 is 6% of $17,123).

Higher Education Tax Credits: Targeting Value, and Interaction... 41

Figure 11. Lifetime Learning Credit and Pell Grant for 16-24 Year Old Single Independent With Some College Enrolling Full-time at a Community College

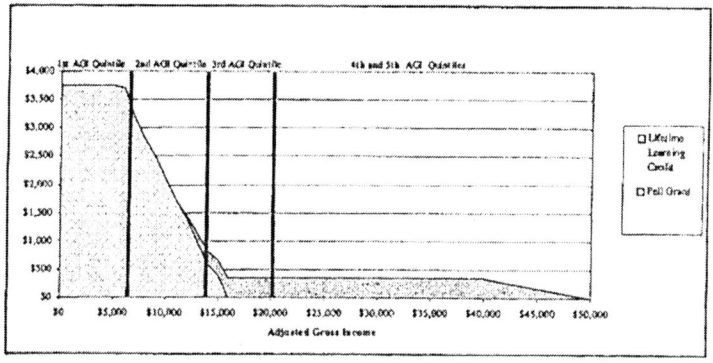

Figure 12. Lifetime Learning Credit and Pell Grant for 16-24 Year Old Single Independent With Some College Enrolling Full-time at a 4-Year Public College

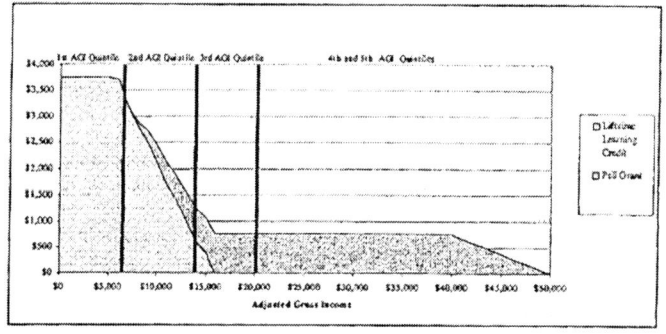

Figure 13. Lifetime Learning Credit and Pell Grant for 16-24 Year Old Single Independent With Some College Enrolling Full-time at a 4-Year Private College

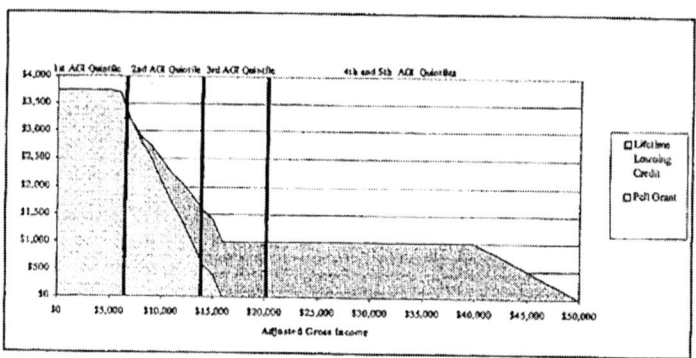

The distribution of Lifetime Learning benefits at all three institutional categories are shown immediately above because, unlike the distribution of the Hope Credit, the distributions at the 4-year public college and 4-year private college are different.[28]

The key points to be made about the distribution of the Lifetime Learning Credit for this student are the following:

- The Lifetime Learning Credit once again is maximized when tuition and fees are high.

- In contrast to the distribution of Lifetime Learning aid to the married independent student, at no point does it offset the loss in Pell Grant assistance experienced by the single independent student as AGI grows.

- The coverage of average tuition and fees across types of institution is the same as described above for the married independent student.

---

[28] This a function of the reimbursement rules for the Lifetime Learning Credit which serve to limit the size of the credit at the 4-year public college level; at the 4-year private college level, tax liability is the limiting factor. In contrast, the Hope reimbursement rules for the first $2,000 in remaining tuition and fees are more generous, as a result tax liability is the limiting factor at both the 4-year public and 4-year private college levels.

Half-time Enrollment

When either of these student cases is enrolled on a half-time basis at a community college or 4-year public college, the Lifetime Learning Credit is reduced largely proportionately. At the 4-year private college, the credit is unaffected by half-time enrollment.

WHAT BENEFITS DO THE CREDITS OFFER AIDED STUDENTS?

This section of the chapter considers the availability of the tax credit benefits to the population of postsecondary students who are receiving federal financial aid from programs authorized by Title IV of the HEA, Title IV aid programs provide loan, grant, and work assistance to students. Title IV programs made an estimated $45.1 billion in federal financial assistance available to students and their families in academic year 1999-2000, constituting roughly two-thirds of all non-tax based direct financial assistance available to support postsecondary students. Title IV aid recipients constitute the largest population of aided students for whom comprehensive background data are available.

With the introduction of higher education tax credits in 1997 as a second major approach toward providing federal student aid, considerable interest has arisen in the complementarity between Title IV grant aid and tax credit assistance. Additionally, as has been discussed throughout this chapter, considerable interest exists in more accurately identifying the population of students eligible to benefit from the tax credits.

The analysis presented below sheds light on the extent to which the students who have traditionally been the focus of federal financial aid—those receiving Title IV aid — are also able to benefit from the tax credits. Additionally it explores the combined targeting of Title IV grant aid and tax credit assistance to these students.

The analysis upon which this portion of the chapter is based utilizes a NFS AS-based tax credit estimation model. This model utilizes comprehensive background information on Title IV recipients (e.g., information on tax liability, adjusted gross income, tuition and fee levels, enrollment and attendance status) which is available in NPSAS[29] and

---

[29] NPSAS data come from a nationally representative sample of approximately 50,000 undergraduate and 12,000 graduate students enrolled in postsecondary institutions in the 1999-2000 academic year.

simulates tax credit benefits available to such students. In some instances, only partial information on a student's characteristic is available in NPSAS. Consequently, some assumptions have been built into the modeling approach. The information presented below on the value and availability of tax credits should therefore be viewed as estimates of what aided students are potentially eligible to receive in tax benefits — and not as precise reflections of actual aid amounts. Readers are encouraged to review the Technical Appendix which outlines the modeling approach and the assumptions embedded within it in greater detail.

It should be noted that tax credit values presented below are being estimated for a national sample of Title IV recipients.[30] In the analysis that follows, these estimated tax credit values are examined in relation to student characteristics and in relation to other financial aid received by students. Findings are presented in a manner that maps estimated tax credit assistance and other available aid across the Title IV aided student population.

Summary of Findings

The analyses presented in the remainder of this section focus on Title IV recipients' access to: tax credits (in aggregate), Hope Credits, Lifetime Learning Credits, and federal obligation-free aid. The primary findings emerging from this examination of tax credit and other assistance available to Title IV recipients include the following:

- Higher education tax credit assistance is widely available to Title IV recipients — roughly 45% of Title IV recipients are eligible to receive tax credits. Students in the lowest income quintile (earning less than $8,176), who are much more likely to be affected by grant aid offsets and the credits' nonrefundability, are much less likely to qualify for tax credit assistance than are students in all other income quintiles.[31]

---

[30] A sample of 23,450 was used for this estimation model. It is comprised of all members of the nationally representative sample of 24,489 Title IV aid recipients (attending a single postsecondary institution in 1999-2000) in NPSAS for which the information needed for tax credit estimation was available.

[31] The income quintile distributions in this portion of the chapter are based on total income in 1998, not AGI as in the preceding portion of the chapter. Income is used here because a significant portion of Title IV recipients do not pay federal income taxes. As a result, AGI values, which are determined within the federal income tax system, are not included in the NPSAS data for those recipients.

- The Hope Credit, available to approximately 38% of those undergraduates receiving Title IV assistance who are in their first 2 years of study, carries a median value of $1,276 — roughly 85% of the maximum potential value of a Hope Credit. Nearly half of the Title IV recipients attending 4-year public, 4-year private, and proprietary schools are eligible for Hope Credits. Median Hope Credit values are above $1,300 for eligible recipients at each of these types of institutions.

- The Lifetime Learning Credit, available to approximately one quarter of the combined pool of undergraduate and graduate Title IV recipients, carries a median value of $556 — roughly 56% of the maximum potential value of a Lifetime Learning Credit. Students attending 4-year public and 4-year private institutions are much more likely to be eligible for a Lifetime Learning Credit than are students attending other institutions. However, the median value of a Lifetime Learning Credit available to those attending 4-year private institutions ($907) is more than double the median value ($411) of the credits available to those attending 4-year public institutions (who are much more likely to have qualified expenses below the maximum allowed under the credit).

- Federal obligation-free aid has become widely available to undergraduate Title IV recipients across all income categories with the introduction of tax credits.[32] Such aid is now available to more than half of the financial aid dependent Title IV recipients in each dependent student income quintile, and more than 90% of financial aid independent Title IV recipients in each independent student income quintile. The percentage of students with at least 10% of tuition and fees covered by available federal obligation-free aid has risen dramatically with the introduction of tax credits.

Higher Education Tax Credits in Aggregate

Figures 14 and 15 and Table 1 present overview information on the higher education tax benefits available to Title IV aid recipients. These figures and Table 1 illustrate, in aggregate, how the credits are targeted to serve the broad population of undergraduate and graduate Title TV aid recipients.

Figure 14. Estimated Percentage of Title IV Aid Recipients Eligible to Receive a Hope or Lifetime fax Credit by Income Quintile, 1999-2000

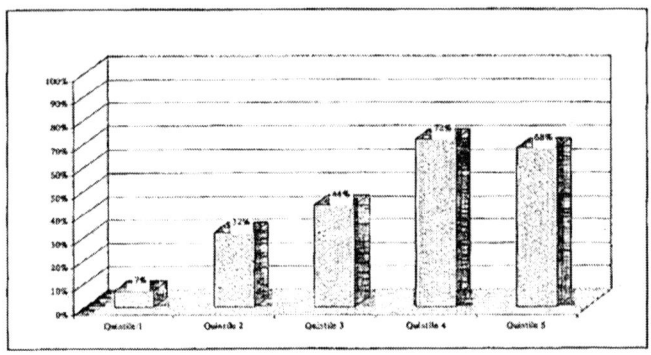

Figure 15. Estimated Median Value of Higher Education Tax Credits Available to Title IV Recipients by Income Quintile, 1999-2000

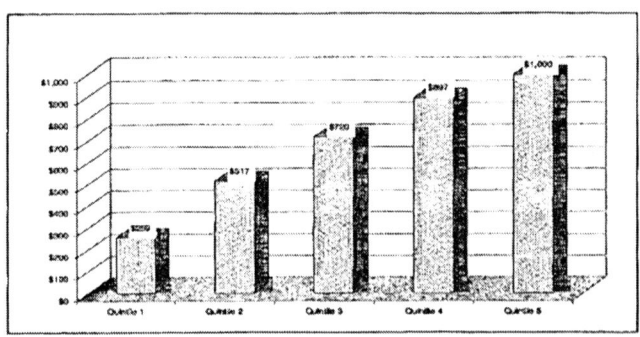

The following key points can be made about the targeting of higher education tax benefits based upon the data presented in these figures and in Table 1 (below):

---

[32] Obligation-free aid (defined in more detail below) is aid that does not have to be repaid or worked for.

- Tax credit assistance has been made available to a large group of Title IV recipients — roughly 45 % qualify for credits which have a median value of almost $800.

- The value of available credits rises steadily across income quintiles, peaking for those in the top quintile. Student eligibility for credits also increases steadily across income quintiles before tapering off a bit for those in the highest quintile (where the benefit phase-out takes effect). It is only students in the lowest income quintile (those earning less than $8,176), who are highly unlikely to qualify for tax credit assistance. These students are much more likely to be affected by grant aid offsets and the credits' nonrefundability than are students in all other income quintiles.

Table 1. Estimated Percentage of Title IV Aid Recipients with Various Characteristics Who Were Eligible to Receive a Hope or Lifetime Learning Tax Credit, and Median Value of the Credit They Were Eligible to Receive, 1999-2000

	Characteristics of Title IV aided student population	Percent eligible for a tax credit	Median tax credit value	Median percent of tuition and fees covered
All Title IV aid recipients	100%	45%	$791	13%
Attendance status				
Full Time	72%	46%	880	12%
Part Time	28%	42%	563	19%
Age				
24 or younger	64%	47%	838	13%
25 or older	36%	41%	701	14%
Sector				
Public 2-year	22%	21%	692	53%
Public 4-year	41%	48%	553	18%
Private 4-year	25%	58%	1000	7%
Proprietary	10%	49%	1000	14%
Other	2%	37%	1227	17%
Dependency				
Dependent	48%	51%	924	13%
Independent	52%	38%	654	14%
Income Quintile				
First (lowest)		7%	259	4%
Second		32%	517	11%
Third		44%	720	14%
Fourth		72%	897	16%
Fifth (highest)		68%	1000	14%

Hope Credits

The Hope Credit was introduced to help ensure students have universal access to the first 2 years of postsecondary education. It is targeted toward undergraduate students enrolled on at least a halt-time basis in a higher education program leading to a degree, certificate, or credential. Table 2 (below) provides comprehensive information on the Hope Credit assistance available to undergraduate Title IV recipients in their first 2 years of study. The following key themes emerge from the data presented in Table 2

- The Hope Credit is available to a relatively large share (approximately 38%) of those undergraduates receiving Tide IV assistance in their first 2 years of study.

- Many of those Title IV recipients eligible to receive Hope Credits come close to obtaining the credit's maximum potential $1,500 value. Hope Credits available to Title IV recipients carry a median value of $1,276—roughly 85% of the maximum potential value of a Hope Credit.

- Nearly half of the Title IV recipients in 4-year public, 4-year private, and proprietary schools are eligible for the Hope Credit Those eligible recipients attending 4-year public, 4-year private, and proprietary schools have median Hope Credit values above $1,300.

Lifetime Learning Credits[33]

The Lifetime Learning Credit was designed to support traditional undergraduate students in any year of study, graduate students, and "lifetime learners" (i.e., those not necessarily pursuing degrees). Like the Hope Credit, the Lifetime Learning Credit was intended to enhance and preserve middle income students' access to higher education. Table 3 presents comprehensive information on the Lifetime Learning Credit assistance available to Title IV

---

[33] Students cannot receive both a Hope Credit and a Lifetime Learning Credit in any given tax year. Students who were technically eligible to receive a Hope Credit or a Lifetime Learning Credit are assumed in this analysis to pursue the more valuable Hope Credit. Thus, they are not treated as being eligible Lifetime Learning Credit recipients.

recipients. Some of the central themes emerging from the data presented in Table 3 include the following:

Table 2. Estimated Percentage of Undergraduate Title IV Aid Recipients in Their First 2 Years of Study Who Were Eligible to Receive a Hope Credit, and Median Value of the Credit They Were Eligible to Receive, 1999-2000

	Characteristics of undergraduate Title IV aided student population in first 2 years of study	Percent eligible for a Hope Credit	Median Hope Credit Value	Median percent of tuition and fees covered
All undergraduate Title IY aid recipients in first 2 years of study				
Attendance status				
Full Time	72%	41%	1375	21%
Part Time	28%	30%	1054	26%
Age				
24 or younger	70%	41%	1338	21%
25 or older	30%	29%	1054	26%
Sector				
Public 2-year	38%	20%	828	57%
Public 4-year	28%	46%	1316	33%
Private 4-year	17%	54%	1500	9%
Proprietary	15%	47%	1500	17%
Other	2%	40%	1500	19%
Dependency				
Dependent	55%	46%	1389	20%
Independent	45%	27%	1030	25%
Income quintile dependent				
First (lowest)		7%	587	10%
Second		26%	747	15%
Third		56%	1364	23%
Fourth		79%	1500	26%
Fifth (highest)		61%	1269	16%
Income quintile independent				
First (lowest)		1%	*	*
Second		15%	388	10%
Third		25%	909	24%
Fourth		32%	1174	24%
Fifth (highest)		62%	1303	30%

Table 3. Estimated Percentage of Title IV Aid Recipients with Various Characteristics Who Were Eligible to Receive Lifetime Learning Tax Credits, and Median Value of the Credit They Were Eligible to Receive, 1999-2000

	Characteristics of Title IV aided student population	Percent eligible for a Lifetime Learning Credit	Median Lifetime Learning Credit Value	Median share of tuition and fees covered
All undergraduate and Title IV aid recipients	100%	25%	$556	10%
Attendance status				
Full Time	72%	25%	627	8%
Part Time	28%	27%	438	14%
Age				
24 or younger				
25 or older				
Sector				
Public 2-year	22%	3%	145	13%
Public 4-year	41%	32%	411	14%
Private 4-year	25%	39%	907	6%
Proprietary	10%	15%	940	12%
Other	2%	6%	406	10%
Dependency				
Dependent	48%	25%	584	9%
Independent	52%	26%	527	11%
Income quintile dependent				
First (lowest)		4%	202	4%
Second		19%	450	7%
Third		32%	547	10%
Fourth		39%	781	13%
Fifth (highest)		27%	498	7%
Income quintile independent				
First (lowest)		3%	259	3%
Second		19%	301	5%
Third		28%	541	11%
Fourth		33%	614	13%
Fifth (highest)		51%	676	13%

- quarter of the combined pool of undergraduate and graduate Title IV recipients, carries a median value of $556 — roughly 56% of the maximum potential value of a Lifetime Learning Credit. Students attending public institutions, who are much more apt to have qualified expenses below the maximum allowed by the credit, have a difficult time maximizing the credit's potential $1,000 value.

- Students attending 4-year public and 4-year private institutions are much more likely to be eligible for a Lifetime Learning Credit than are students attending other institutions. Approximately 39% of Title IV recipients attending 4-year private schools are eligible to receive Lifetime Learning Credits, which have a median value of $907 for this group. Roughly one third of Title IV recipients in 4-year public institutions are eligible to receive Lifetime Learning Credits, which have a median value of $411. Lifetime Learning Credits are not very accessible to Title IV recipients attending 2-year public institutions (an estimated 3%).

Distribution of Federal Obligation-Free Aid

This section of the chapter considers federal student grant aid, such as the Pell Grant, and the federal education tax credits in tandem. The combined targeting of federal grant aid and education tax credits is of widespread interest to policymakers concerned about federal financial support for postsecondary students. Both sources of aid aim to promote postsecondary education access by covering postsecondary education expenses during periods of enrollment. Additionally, the credits and grant aid share a fundamentally important feature — they are federal "obligation-free" assistance.[34] That is, neither of these kinds of aid carries a post-award or post-receipt non-academic obligation. Unlike loans, they do not have to be repaid. Unlike work study awards, they require no work. As federal obligation-free assistance, grants and education tax credits are the most desirable forms of federal aid from the recipient's perspective. As a result, it is important to consider how the advent of the education tax credits has affected the distribution of federal obligation-free assistance.

"Generally available" federal obligation-free aid is disbursed in the form of grants and tax credits. Prior to the introduction of the Hope and Lifetime

---

[34] Subsequent references in this chapter to obligation-free assistance are references to either federal student aid grants, the postsecondary education tax credits, or both sources of aid.

Learning Credits, all such aid was disbursed as need-sensitive grant aid (i.e., Pell Grants and Supplemental Educational Opportunity Grants - SEOGs). The introduction of tax credits greatly expanded the pool of individuals eligible to receive federal obligation-free aid.

Table 4 offers a depiction of the generally available obligation-free aid available to Title IV recipients and the extent to which such aid defrays the cost of tuition and fees. Figures 16 and 17 provide information on the composition of this kind of aid; specifically, they illustrate the relative role being played by grants and tax credits in assisting students in varying income quintiles. The following key points can be made based upon the data presented below.

Table 4. Estimated Percentage of Undergraduate Title IV Recipients by Income Quintile Who Were Eligible to Receive Federal Obligation-Free Aid in 1999-2000

	Percent eligible to receive federal obligation-free aid	Median amount available	Median percent of tuition and fees covered
Income quintile Dependent			
First (lowest)	97%	3075	100%
Second	97%	2174	68%
Third	90%	1224	23%
Fourth	84%	1000	19%
Fifth (highest)	54%	682	10%
Income quintile independent			
First (lowest)	95%	2975	102%
Second	98%	1700	83%
Third	95%	1563	81%
Fourth	98%	1500	84%
Fifth (highest)	94%	1000	31%

- Federal obligation-free aid is now widely available to Title IV recipients across income categories. This aid is being made available to more than half of the top income quintile of dependent students, and the median share of tuition and fees covered by such aid available to these students is 10%. In all other dependent and independent student income quintiles, more than 80% of students are eligible to receive federal obligation-free aid, and the median share of tuition and fees covered by such aid ranges from roughly 20% to more than 100%.

- For dependent students, grants are the dominant form of federal obligation-free aid for those in the two lower income quintiles. A fairly even balance exists between available grant and tax credit assistance for those in the middle quintile ($32,812 - $50,702), and tax credits are the dominant source of this kind of aid for those in the upper quintiles. For independent students, grants are the dominant source of this aid for each income quintile except the highest quintile (earning $27,661 and above). For students in this quintile, a balance exists between available grant aid and tax credit assistance.

Figure 16. Estimated Composition of Aggregate Federal Obligation-Free Aid Made Available to Dependent Undergraduate Title IV Aid Recipients by Income Quintile, 1999-2000

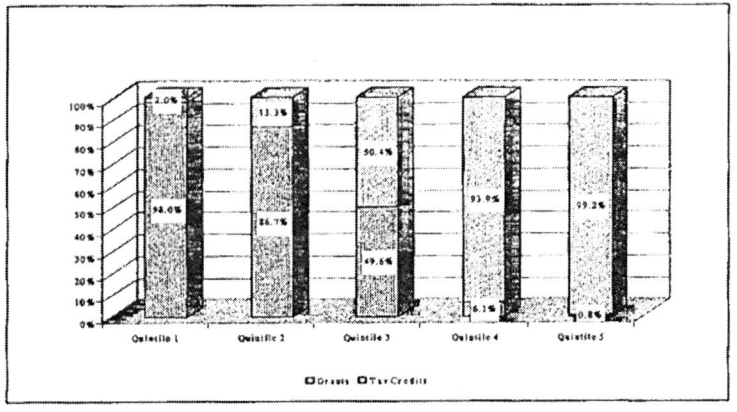

Figure 17. Estimated Composition of Aggregate Federal Obligation-Free Aid Made Available to Independent Undergraduate Title IV Aid Recipients by Income Quintile, 1999-2000

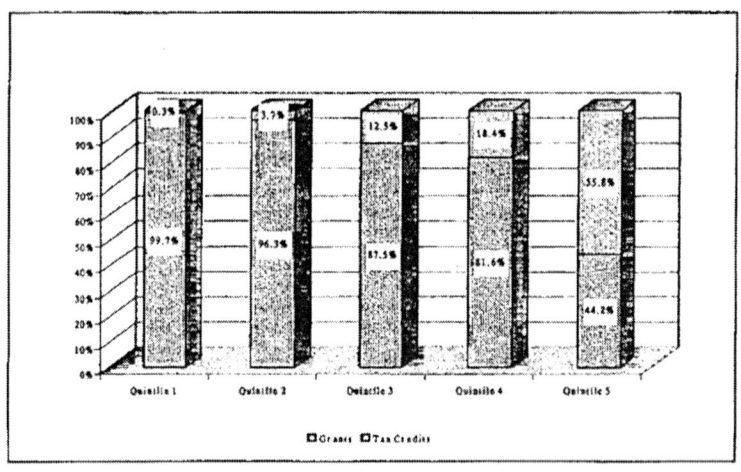

How Has the Introduction of Tax Credits Affected the Targeting of Federal Obligation-Free Aid?

Prior to the introduction of tax credits, the general prevailing philosophy in the federal student aid effort, rooted in the basic tenets of the original HEA of 1965, was to first award grants to cover the higher education costs of those with high levels of need, and if necessary, supplement grants with subsidized loans. The aid approach for middle-income students centered on providing subsidized borrowing opportunities.

With the introduction of the Hope and Lifetime Learning Credits, two new sources of obligation-free aid became available that serve middle income-students. This expansion of the role played by such aid within the federal student aid effort has sparked debate about how obligation-free aid is currently targeted, how the role of such aid has changed, and about the role this aid should play within the overarching federal aid effort.

The figures below have been produced to shed some light on how the targeting of obligation-free aid across income brackets has changed. Figures 18 to 23 illustrate the targeting of this aid in 1995-1996 and 1999-2000, a period immediately prior to the introduction of the tax credits and a period shortly after the tax credits became available (in 1998).[35] The 1995-1996 data reflect the estimated distribution of Pell and SEOG awards in the 1995-1996 academic year. The 1999-2000 data reflect the estimated distribution of federal grant aid and also include the estimated Hope and Lifetime Learning Credit assistance made available.[36]

Shifts in the targeting of obligation-free aid displayed in Figures 18 and 19 can be thought of as largely reflecting the effects of the tax credits. This is because few changes were enacted in federal grant eligibility requirements during this time period. Shifts in the percent of tuition and fees covered by obligation-free aid depicted in Figures 20 through 23 can be thought of as reflecting both increases in Pell awards and the introduction of tax assistance for those in lower income quintiles, and as primarily reflecting the effects of tax credits for those in higher income quintiles.

The central themes emerging from the data presented in the figures below include the following:

- When Title IV recipients are examined by income quintile in academic years 1995-1996 and 1999-2000, it becomes apparent that targeting of federal obligation-free aid has changed dramatically. Students in the upper three income quintiles had far greater access to such aid in 1999-2000 than in 1995-1996. This trend is most strongly accentuated in the 4th and 5th income quintiles for dependent students. The majority of dependent Title IV recipients in these quintiles (84% and 54%, respectively) in 1999-2000 had access to federal obligation-free aid.

- The incidence of Title IV recipients having at least 10% of their tuition and fees covered by generally available[37] obligation-free aid has grown considerably over the period. This is most evident for dependent students in the 4th and 5th quintiles whose access to such federal aid covering one-tenth of their tuition rose to 60% (from 7%) and to 27% (from 0%), respectively.

---

[35] "Generally available" aid is available to students attending eligible institutions regardless of the specific kind of postsecondary education being pursued.
[36] Undergraduate students are the focus of this examination because federal grant assistance (the only form of generally available federal obligation-free aid available prior to 1998) is only provided to undergraduates.
[37] The 1995-1996 data utilized for this analysis are from the 1995-1996 NPSAS. The 1999-2000 data are from the 1999-2000 NPSAS.

Figure 18. Estimated Percentage of Undergraduate Dependent
Title IV Aid Recipients by Income Quintile Eligible for
Federal Obligation-Free Aid, 1995-1996 and 1999-2000

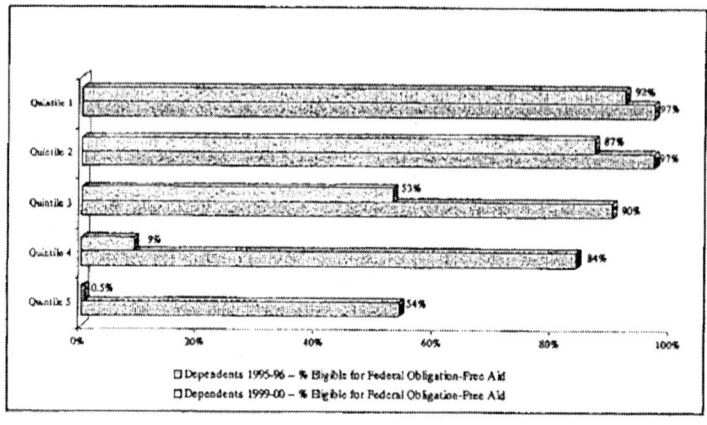

Figure 19. Estimated Percentage of Undergraduate Independent
Title IV Aid Recipients by Income Quintile Eligible for Federal
Obligation-Free Aid, 1995-1996 and 1999-2000

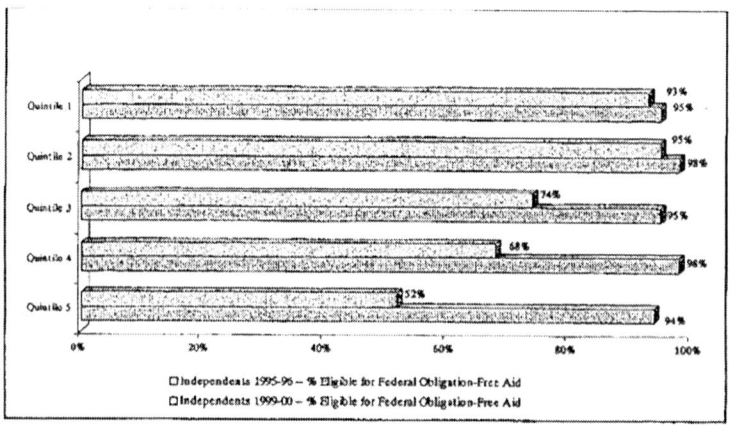

Figure 20. Estimated Percentage of Dependent Undergraduate Title IV Aid Recipients by Income Quintile Having At Least 10% of Tuition and Fees Covered by Available Federal Obligation-Free Aid, 1995-1996 and 1999-2000

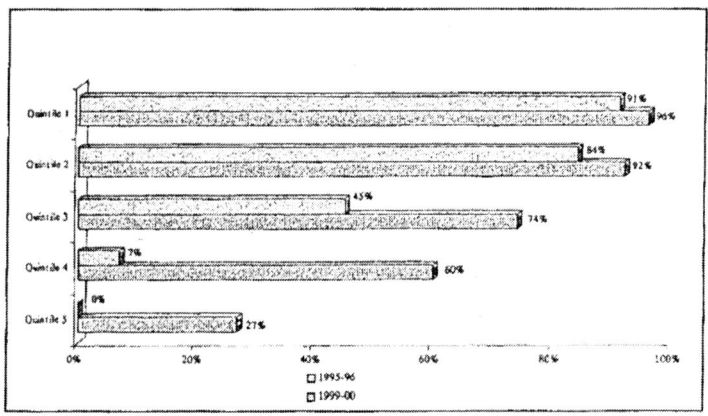

Figure 21. Estimated Percentage of Dependent Undergraduate Title IV Aid Recipients by Income Quintile Having At Least One-Fourth of Tuition and Fees Covered by Available Federal Obligation-Free Aid, 1995-1996 and 1999-2000

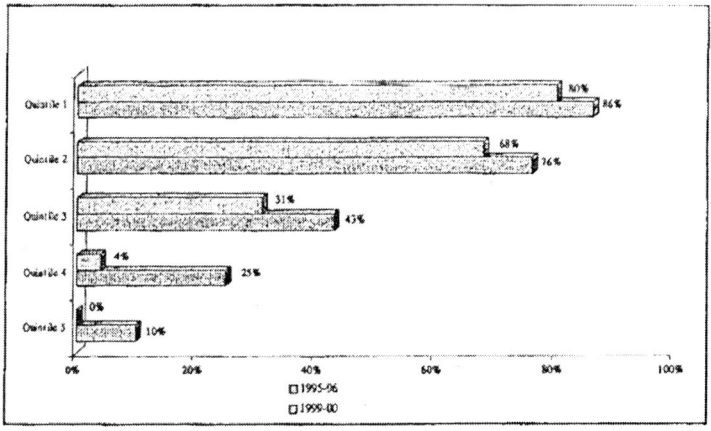

Figure 22. Estimated Percentage of Independent Undergraduate Title IV Aid Recipients by Income Quintile Having At Least 10% of Tuition and Fees Covered by Available Federal Obligation-Free Aid, 1995-1996 and 1999-2000

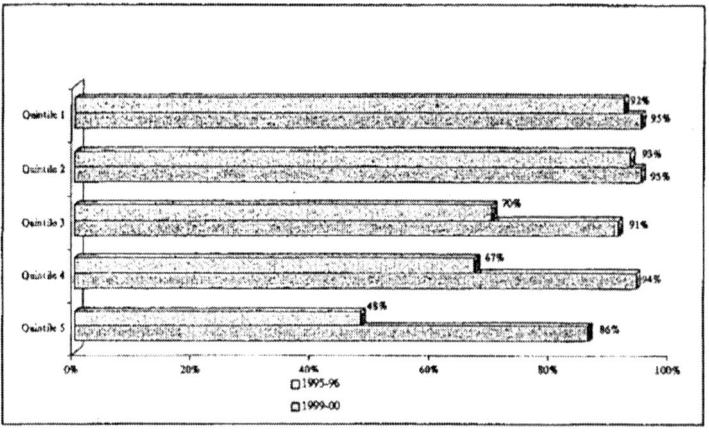

Figure 23. Estimated Percentage of Independent Undergraduate Title IV Aid Recipients by Income Quintile Having At Least One-Fourth of Tuition and Fees Covered by Available Federal Obligation-Free Aid, 1995-1996 and 1999-2000

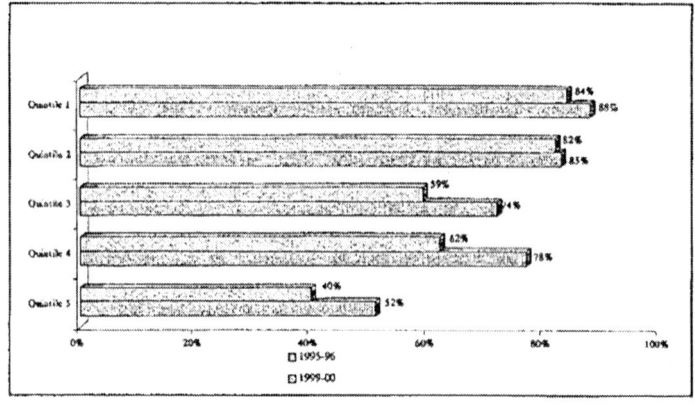

WHY DO THE CREDITS ALLOT THEIR BENEFITS THE WAY THEY DO AND HOW WOULD PROPOSED CHANGES AFFECT THAT ALLOTMENT?

As shown by the preceding analyses of estimated distributions of the education tax credit benefits to potential students and aided undergraduates, the credits are primarily available to middle-income students. Although under some circumstances they do reach down to lower income students, they are not available to the poorest students under any circumstances. Students maximize their benefits from the tax credits where tuition and fees are relatively high. At such institutions, this works to increase the amount of the benefit and extend the coverage of the benefit further down the income scale. Further, across some income ranges, students may receive grant aid, such as Pell Grants, as well as an education credit. This may boost the aggregate amount of federal obligation-free aid that these students receive above what they would otherwise receive in the absence of the credits.

Why do the credits allot their benefits in this manner? As was discussed earlier, the credits have several award rules that dictate eligibility and benefit amount. These include:

- the education costs that may be covered by the credits,
- the grant aid offset,
- the reimbursement rules (with their caps on the maximum credit)
- nonrefundability, and
- phase-out rates.

It is useful to consider the award rules to have an implicit order of application — the order in which they are listed above. Initially, one must determine which postsecondary education expenses are eligible to be covered by the credits. If grant aid, such as the Pell Grant, fully offsets the covered costs, there are no eligible costs for which a credit might be claimed. Where eligible costs exceed grant aid, there are remaining costs to be covered by the credits. At that juncture, the reimbursement rules applied to those remaining costs dictate the potential maximum credit that can be claimed. The nonrefundability rule determines what portion, if any, of that potential maximum credit can actually be claimed, barring a reduction due to the phase-out rates.

There is interest in the Congress in changing the distribution of these education tax credit benefits and bills have been introduced that would modify some of these award rules.[38] Each of these factors can exert some influence on who can claim a credit and how much they claim, but each is not likely to have an equal effect on different groups of potential claimants. Changes to certain of the award rules are likely to benefit middle-income and higher income students; changes to others hold out the promise of making the tax credit benefits available to more low-income students, including the poorest students.[39] Perhaps one of the most important features of the award rules for any consideration of changes in the distribution of the tax benefits is that they can interact This is inherent in the order of application just described. The interaction among multiple award rules may particularly affect the benefits for low-income students. For those students, especially in lower priced institutions, changes to only one of the award rules without concurrent modification of others will not expand the benefits they may receive.

For upper middle-income and higher income students, nonrefundability is not an issue since these students are likely to have sufficient tax liability to claim a credit. Further, the grant aid offset may be inconsequential for the many who are unlikely to receive substantial amounts of grant aid. Expanding the credits to cover other costs, such as room and board, or books, or, indeed, the entire cost of attendance, while maintaining all other current rules, would have an impact on such students only if they are attending relatively low-priced institutions, particularly community colleges. For instance, the average tuition and fees in the community college sector, are not sufficiently high for the maximum Hope Credit to be claimed. Allowing the credits to cover all other expenses in addition to tuition and fees would boost the Hope Credit for such students to the maximum allowable. Raising the credit caps while making no other changes would particularly benefit students enrolled at 4-year private institutions where, as a result of higher tuition and fee levels, the caps limit the amount of tax benefit that can be claimed. For high-income students, the phase-out rates also directly limit benefits (e.g., at AGIs above $100,000 for those filing a joint tax return, no benefit is available).

---

[38] See, for example, H.R. 414, H.R. 928, H.R. 1777, H.R. 2219, H.R. 2482, S. 687, and S. 888.
[39] Of the award rules delineated above, changes to the grant aid offset appear to be the most problematic from a policy perspective given that such changes could raise the possibility of a student receiving grant aid and a tax benefit for the same postsecondary education expenditures. As a consequence, although we identify where this award rule might affect a student's tax credit, we do not simulate its modification or removal.

The primary limiting factor for middle-income students, particularly those attending relatively high priced institutions, appears to be the reimbursement rules and their caps. As with higher income students, expanding coverage of the credits beyond tuition and fees while maintaining the current reimbursement rules will do little to increase the tax benefits. Nonrefundability and the grant aid offset may affect some students at the lower end of this income group.

Possibly more so than for any other income group, low-income students' eligibility for the credits and the level of benefit they may claim are primarily a function of an interaction among all of these award rules, save for the phase-out rates. This appears to be particularly true at lower priced institutions. This interaction is explored more fully below.

Interplay of Coverage of Costs and Nonrefundability for Low-Income Students

In an effort to illustrate the complex interaction of the award rules for low-income students, and in particular the lowest income students, the impact of the interplay of two rules—nonrefundability and coverage of costs—on the size of the Hope Credits at the community college level is explored here. At these institutions which charge relatively low tuition, a third rule — the grant aid offset — works in tandem with the cost coverage rule to limit benefits.

This analysis provides a context for considering whether and how the credits might be modified to extend the Hope Credit further down the income range, possibly responding to concerns raised by some analysts that the Hope Credit will have a limited impact on access because it does not benefit the families for whom financial barriers are the primary impediment to postsecondary enrollment.[40] The changes addressed here are intended primarily to extend to the lowest income students at the community college level the tax benefits received by their higher income colleagues, not to increase significantly the size of the benefits across the full income spectrum.

The importance of the order in which the award rules are applied for low-income students at relatively low-priced schools is that no one change appears to be sufficient to extend the tax credit benefits down to the lowest income student. Given that at low-income levels, students and their families are unlikely to have much if any tax liability, attention is often likely to be focused on nonrefundability as the barrier to receipt of tax credit benefits. But, as shown below, that is not the case where the covered costs are relatively low.

The following figures based on the case simulation model show how two award rules — the coverage of cost rule and nonrefundability rule — affect the size of the Hope Credit, independently and together, for the single independent student considered earlier enrolled at a community college.[41] The first figure below depicts the distribution under current law (nonrefundable Hope Credit with the current cost coverage rule). The next figures show, respectively, the impact of expanding the coverage of costs to the full cost of attendance while maintaining all other award rules; making the credit refundable only; or making both of these changes.

Figure 24. Hope Credit and Pell Grant for 16-24 Year Old Single Independent High School Graduate Enrolling Full-time at a Community College

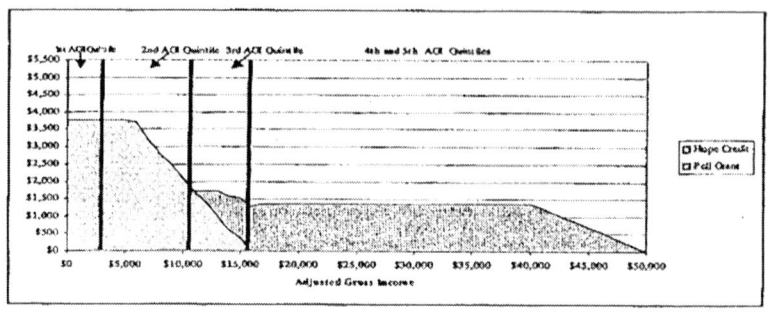

For this student, expanding eligible costs to the full cost of attendance extends the Hope Credit further down the income scale, boosting aid for the upper end of the 2nd AGI quintile (Figure 25). At these income levels, there is tax liability that can be used to claim the credit. This change also boosts

---

[40] Wolanin, Thomas R. Rhetoric and Reality: Effects and Consequences of the HOPE Scholarship. The Institution for Higher Education Policy, Working Paper, April 2001.

[41] As noted above, the precise interplay of the award rules will differ from case to case. The single independent student at a community college was chosen for this analysis because this type of student at this institution appears to realize less Hope Credit benefit than other students considered in this chapter. As a result, expanding tax credit assistance to such a student may be an important objective for efforts to modify the education credits. These figures have an expanded Y-axis ($0 to $5,500) compared to earlier figures ($0 to $4,000) to accommodate the increased aggregate level of assistance that may be realized.

the maximum credit available (from $ 1,369 to $ 1,500 — previously, the reimbursement rule interacted with the low average tuition and fee level at the community college to restrict the maximum Hope Credit). But, the credit does not reach the lowest income levels, where there is no tax liability.

Figure 25. Hope Credit and Pell Grant for 16-24 Year Old Single Independent High School Graduate Enrolling Full-time at a Community College — Eligible Costs are the Cost of Attendance

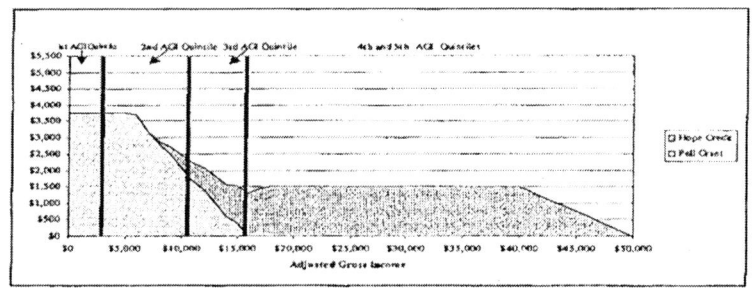

Figure 26. Hope Credit and Pell Grant for 16-24 Year Old Single Independent High School Graduate Enrolling Full-time at a Community College — Refundable Credit

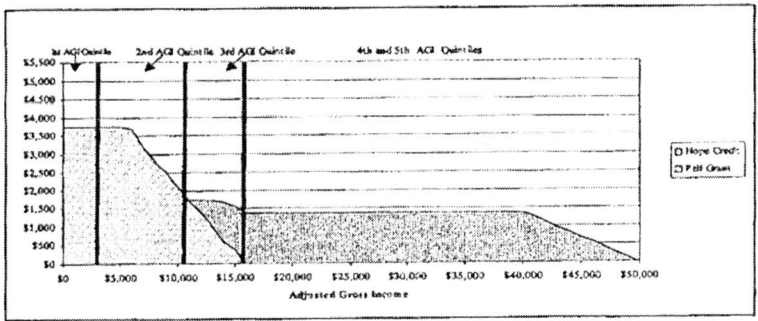

Figure 27. Hope Credit and Pell Grant for 16-24 Year Old Single Independent High School Graduate Enrolling Full-time at a Community College — Refundable Credit and Eligible Costs are the Cost of Attendance

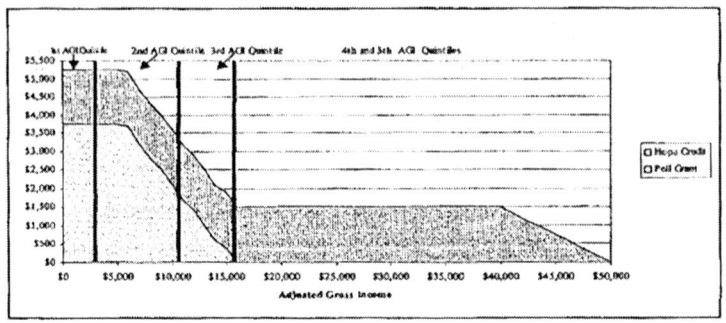

Alternatively, making the credit refundable, while leaving the current cost coverage rule in effect, has a barely perceptible impact on the distribution of aid because, for the lowest income student, the Pell Grant amount more than covers tuition and fee charges (Figure 26). The cost coverage rule (coupled with the grant aid offset) is curbing the amount of remaining tuition and fees for the credit to reimburse.

Only when a refundable Hope Credit is available and eligible costs are expanded to the full cost of attendance, can the absolute maximum Hope Credit of $1,500 be claimed throughout the AGI range from $0 to $40,000 (Figure 27). This combination of changes extends the Hope Credit all the way down the income spectrum to the lowest-income student, and also slightly boosts the credit that higher income students are eligible to claim.[42]

Finally, we would note that expanding federal aid to low-income students to address access needs might be accomplished, alternatively, through changes to federal grant aid programs, particularly the Pell Grant program. An exploration of such changes is beyond the scope of this chapter, but they would include such modifications as an increase in the minimum Pell Grant which would more fully focus Pell Grant funding on the poorest students (by reducing higher income students' eligibility for grants).

---

[42] The pattern in the distribution of benefits simulated in these figures is similar to what the distribution of benefits would be for this type of student at a 4-year public institution (at the average tuition and fees and costs of attendance at that kind of institution), hi contrast, at a 4-year private college with substantially higher tuition and fee charges, making the Hope Credit refundable with no simultaneous change in the cost coverage rule would extend the tax credit benefit down to the lowest income student.

CONCLUSIONS

The Hope and Lifetime Learning Credits are now major components of the federal effort to promote access to postsecondary education. Several significant findings emerge from the preceding analysis of the potential distribution of these tax benefits to out-of-school young adults and to federally aided undergraduates.

The Hope Credit provides a substantial benefit to recipients and spreads these benefits relatively broadly. By design, the credit targets the bulk of its benefits to middle- and upper middle-income students. But, it also reaches down the income scale and provides assistance to some low-income students. As a result, the Hope Credit overlaps with the other major source of federal obligation-free aid, the Pell Grants.

In contrast, the Lifetime Learning Credit provides relatively little benefit even to the populations on which it is targeted. With many of the same award rules as the Hope Credit, it directs most of its benefits to middle- and upper middle-income students. But, given the Lifetime Learning Credit's reimbursement rule (20% of qualified expenses with a $1,000 benefit cap), it is worth significantly less than the Hope Credit. Its reimbursement rule also means that a student maximizes his or her Lifetime Learning Credit by attending higher priced institutions.

The advent and growth of the Hope and Lifetime Learning Credits have dramatically shifted the focus of federal obligation-free aid for postsecondary education attendance. Previously, such federal aid was principally need-based aid targeted to the lowest income students. The education tax credits provide their benefits without regard to the traditional federal need analysis system and financial aid packaging procedures on college campuses. As a consequence, federal obligation-free aid is now available, not only to low-income students, but to the broad expanse of middle- and upper middle-income students.

Efforts to change the targeting of the tax credits and their interaction with traditional federal student aid are complicated by the interaction of the various award rules of these financial resources. Single changes to the award rules may benefit only some income groups and not others. In particular, expansion of these tax benefits to the lowest income students attending lower priced institutions appears to depend upon making changes to multiple award rules.

TECHNICAL APPENDIX

This appendix briefly describes some of the important technical features of the estimation models used in this analysis.

Case Simulation Model

The case simulation model used for the analysis of the potential distribution of tax benefits to the out-of-school population consists of two models — a Pell Grant estimation model and a federal income tax model.

Pell Grant Estimation Model

For each case being simulated, the Pell Grant estimation model calculated the appropriate EFC and applied the Pell Grant award rules to determine the size of the Pell Grant for that case at any particular level of AGI.

Certain assumptions were made to facilitate the analysis. As noted earlier, it was assumed that the rule determining the size of the Pell Grant for every case was: maximum appropriated Pell Grant minus EFC. Further, it was assumed for each case that assets did not exceed the appropriate asset-related allowances specified for the EFC calculation. Therefore, no contribution was expected from assets for any case considered here. Assumptions about family size are delineated earlier in the text.

The EFC allowances, assessment rates, and other factors used in the Pell Grant estimation model applied to award year 2001-2002 when the maximum appropriated Pell Grant was $3,750. For that award year, the EFC calculation was based on 2000 calendar year income. The AGI levels considered by the federal income tax model were for 2001 as were the levels depicted in the various figures in this chapter for the out-of-school population. As a result, the AGI levels used for the EFC calculations were deflated from the 2001 levels, using the change in the annual average CPI-U from 2000 to 2001 of 2.8%.

Federal Income Tax Model

The federal income tax model utilized for this analysis applied 2001 income tax rules to the cases being simulated, maintaining all of the relevant characteristics utilized in estimating the Pell Grant. Further, based on the estimated tax liability for each case, the model determined the level of the

Hope or Lifetime Learning Credits. To facilitate these estimates, it was assumed that none of the cases simulated here claimed the foreign tax credit, the credit for child and dependent care, or the credit for care of the elderly or the disabled.

The income tax model calculated the education tax credit using the appropriate qualified tuition and fee expenses. For that calculation, it was necessary to make the analysis specific to a particular academic year. To that end, it was assumed that the student paid for his or her 2001-2002 postsecondary education entirely during calendar year 2001. As a consequence, the estimated Pell Grant, which is also for 2001-2002, can be used in the application of the grant aid offset rule for the education tax credits.

Survey Data Model

Methodology

The estimated Hope and Lifetime Learning Credits available to 1999-2000 Title IV aid recipients shown in this chapter have been generated though a NPSAS-based tax credit estimation model. This model utilizes comprehensive background information on Title IV recipients which is available in NPSAS (e.g., information on their tax liability, adjusted gross income, tuition and fee levels, enrollment and attendance status) and simulates tax credit benefits available to such students. The estimates generated through this model are based on some assumptions. The primary operating assumptions built into this Hope and Lifetime Learning Credit estimation model are discussed below.

Time Period Assumptions (reconciling differences in benefit year and academic year)

The model assumes that the tax credits claimed in the 1999 calendar year tax will be claimed against tuition and fee expenses for the entire 1999-2000 academic year. This is allowable under the benefit as long as payments are made in calendar year 1999 (i.e., we are assuming tuition for courses beginning in January is paid in December).

The credits are thus treated as aid received for academic year 1999-2000 tuition expenses and analyzed in relation to the rest of the aid package received in the 1999-2000 academic year. The credits are also analyzed in relation to tuition and fees paid in the 1999-2000 academic year.

Assumptions Related to Tax Liability

Information on tax liability used in the model is taken from the 1998 return as reported by the student or parent on the Free Application for Federal Student Aid (FAFSA) for 1999-2000. These tax liability data have been inflation adjusted to 1999 dollars, and then treated as 1999 tax liability figures in the model.

Additionally, an adjustment was made to address a discrepancy in the tax liability figure provided on FAFSA and the tax liability figure needed to calculate tax credits. Basically, the figure provided on FAFSA can appropriately be thought of as a "final" tax liability figure (i.e., total tax liability after the value of all tax credits — even Hope and Lifetime Learning Credits — have been subtracted). Whereas, the tax liability figure needed to determine whether one has sufficient tax liability for Hope and Lifetime calculations is an "almost final" tax liability figure produced after some but not all tax credits are subtracted from one's available tax liability. The effect of using the "final" as opposed to "almost final" tax liability information in an estimation model could be to understate the value of the benefit some students are eligible to receive (i.e., those students with limited tax liability for the credit to offset).

For those cases, deemed through analyses to be adversely affected by the missing information, tax liability values have been restored using information available elsewhere in the FAFSA. These adjustments have affected the estimated tax credit values of 3.2% of the population studied.[43]

Assumptions Related to Number of Higher Education Credits Claimed

It is possible that a family with more than one postsecondary student may claim more than one higher education tax credit. If their tax liability is

---

[43] To address this, we have added the FAFSA Worksheet B values to the FAFSA tax liability figures. FAFSA Worksheet B contains the aggregate value of education (Hope and Lifetime) credits claimed during the 1998 tax year by the tax filer, and this adjustment is done to restore the tax liability levels against which the filer claimed 1998 education credits. The median amount added through this adjustment was $1,022.

It should be noted though that Worksheet B values reported on FAFSA reflect more than just education credit values. They also reflect child support payments being made for a child living outside of one's household, taxable earnings from Federal Work Study or other need-based work-study programs, AmeriCorps awards, and grant aid in excess of tuition and fees. A composite number reflecting all of these values is reported on FAFSA. Because we add this composite value to restore tax liability values, it can be assumed that we have inflated actual liability levels for some parents and students. In such instances, we may exaggerate the tax credit benefit available. We took care in restoring values only for those with sufficient incomes to qualify for credits sufficient to capture at least some of the value of one credit, but not sufficient to enable the filer to capture the value of multiple credits, essentially the value of each credit to the taxpayer is reduced. We estimate that roughly 2% of the population studied are at risk of having some of the value of their credit "reduced" by the presence of another credit-eligible family member. Tax credit estimates presented in this chapter make no adjustments for this possible occurrence.

Assumptions Related to Dependency

In this model we assume that individuals who are independent for student aid purposes are independent tax filers, and those who are dependent for student aid purposes are treated as dependents for another filer's (presumably a parent's) tax form. We have no actual information about how closely tax filing dependency status mirrors student aid filing dependency status. Thus, we cannot estimate the extent to which this assumption detracts from the precision of our modeling. The likely effects of having made inaccurate assumptions about the tax status of some dependent students is that we have probably overestimated their tax credit eligibility (by relying on their parents' tax liability in our estimates as opposed to the students' tax liability). The effect of having made inaccurate assumptions about the tax status of some independent students is that we have probably underestimated their tax credit eligibility (by relying on their own tax liability in our estimates as opposed to their parents' tax liability).

INDEX

A

adjusted gross income (AGI), 2, 5-9, 12, 14, 26-31, 33-36, 42-44, 62, 64, 66, 67

B

bachelor's degree (BA), 26, 27, 38, 40
beneficiaries, 9, 12
benefit size, 13
Bureau of the Census, 25, 26

C

Case Simulation Modeling, 25
college access, 24
college costs, 18
condition for enrollment, 5, 30
cost of education, 25
Current Population Survey (CPS), 25-27, 29, 38

D

Department of Education (ED), 4, 17
dependent exemptions, 14
dependent students, 52, 53, 55, 69
drug possession, 4

E

education credits, 9, 14, 21, 28, 62, 68
education expenses, vii, 1, 3, 5, 7, 8, 15, 21, 22, 28, 30, 51, 59
education tax credits, 1, 10, 21, 22, 29, 45, 46
educational benefits, 5
eligible student(s), 4, 5
expected family contribution (EFC), 18, 28, 29, 33, 66

F

family composition, 25
Federal Family Education Loan, 3
federal financial aid, 9
federal financial assistance for postsecondary education, 2
federal income tax credits, 2
federal income tax system, 3, 16, 18
federal obligation-free aid, 45, 52
federal postsecondary obligation-free aid, 22
federal student aid, 18, 19, 23, 26, 43, 51, 54, 65
felony conviction, 4

financial aid officers, 3, 17, 19, 20
Free Application for Federal Student
   Aid (FAFSA), 68

G

graduate enrollment, 7, 8
grant aid offset, 27, 30, 33, 59-61, 64, 67
gross income, 5, 6

H

Half-time Enrollment, 37, 43
HEA Title IV, 3, 19
Higher Education Act (HEA), vii, 3, 18, 21, 23, 43, 54
Higher education tax benefits, 9
higher education, 2-7, 9-17, 20
higher income students, 60, 61, 64
Hope credit, 1, 2, 4-6, 8, 11-14
Hope Scholarship (tax) Credit, 2, 4, 8
human capital investments, 9

I

Income and Tax Liability, 13
income thresholds, 1, 5, 6, 14, 30
inflation, 4, 5, 6, 8, 9, 14, 30, 68
Internal Revenue Service (IRS), 3, 10, 17, 18, 23

J

job skills, 6, 30

L

Lifetime Learning credit, 5, 6, 10-13, 15
Lifetime Learning tax credit, 1, 2

M

marginal tax rate, 7, 8, 12, 13, 15
Married Independent Student(s), 32, 38
maximum value, 2, 12, 14

N

National Postsecondary Student Aid
   Study (NPSAS), 25, 43, 44, 55, 67
net financial benefit, 20
nonrefundability rule, 59, 62
nonrefundable tax credit, 2, 4, 5
non-taxable, 5, 15, 30
nontraditional students, 11

P

Pell Grant(s), 3, 5, 16, 26, 28-42, 51, 59, 62-64, 66, 67
postsecondary education, 2, 3, 7-11, 14- 16, 20
postsecondary institutions, 3, 5, 43
private institutions, 15, 45, 51, 60
provisions, 1, 7, 12, 19

Q

qualified expenses, 2, 5, 7, 8, 11, 12, 15, 17, 19, 30, 33, 45, 51, 65
Qualified Tuition and Related
   Expenses, 15
qualified tuition, 4, 5, 13, 28, 67

S

scholarships, 5, 18
Single Independent Student, 34
standard deductions, 14
student financial support, 16
Supplemental Educational
   Opportunity Grants (SEOGs), 52
Survey Data Modeling, 25

T

tax benefit(s), 1-3, 7, 9, 10, 12, 14-21, 24, 27, 44-46, 60, 61, 65, 66
tax credit assistance, 25, 43, 44, 47, 53, 62
tax credits, 3, 9, 12-15, 17-20
tax deduction, 1, 2, 6, 7, 8, 10-15, 19
tax liability, 4, 7, 8, 13, 14, 16, 19, 25, 30, 35, 37, 42, 43, 60, 62, 66-69
tax provisions, 2, 3, 15, 17, 19
tax savings, 7, 11
taxpayers, 2, 4-6, 8, 11, 12, 14, 15, 17, 18, 30
The Economic Growth and Tax Relief Reconciliation Act of 2001, 1, 6
the federal income tax system, 2, 44
The Hope credit, 5, 10, 11
The Hope Scholarship tax credit, 1
the tax system, 3, 16, 19
The Taxpayer Relief Act of 1997, 1, 2, 21, 22
tuition and fees, 2, 4, 15, 20, 28, 30-37, 40, 42, 45, 47, 49, 50, 52, 55, 59-61, 64, 67, 68

U

U.S. Department of Education (ED), 4
undergraduate education, 4, 8, 13
undergraduate students, 10, 48

W

work aid, 3